Praise for
THE LOG CABIN YEARS

"With *The Log Cabin Years*, Cindy Ross has joined an elite order of wilderness homesteading writers that would include Helen and Scott Nearing (*Living the Good Life*), Richard Proenneke (*One Man's Wilderness*), Allan and Mary Mackie (*Building With Logs*), Calvin Rutstrum (*The Wilderness Cabin*), Helen Hoover (*A Place in the Woods*), and Anne LaBastille (*Woodswoman*). Making use of warm, often humorous anecdotes, Ms. Ross gently inquires, in effect: Why would anyone want to pilot the complex, arduous process of constructing a permanent dwelling of whole logs? This begs the question of relationship dynamics: How will a married couple with a handful of occasional volunteer helpers successfully get along with one another during the long, stressful period it takes to complete such a daunting undertaking? Among the many practical, helpful tips included in the book is this gem: 'The skills you learn while navigating your relationship will mean just as much to your future happiness as a solid, beautiful home.' I predict that *The Log Cabin Years* will stand out as a classic in the American back-to-the-land literary genre of the late twentieth century."

—RON BRODIGAN, log house building teacher, restoration consultant

"*The Log Cabin Years* is one part how-to and two or three parts why and wherefore and wow. In this truly captivating read, we get a sense of the setbacks, the trials, the tribulations, and the deep, enduring satisfaction of building your own home—a home that fits the Thoreauvian ideal of a life welllived. Working with her husband Todd, Ross discovers that building a log cabin turns out to be a 'training ground' for marriage and a life together, one sawed, peeled, and hoisted log at a time. Among the book's many attractions are Ross's lovely and detailed drawings as she literally sketches in all the steps of the building process. It's a pleasure all its own, as rich as the pleasures of the text itself, to follow the story told by the sketches in the book until the cabin, taking shape job by job, emerges by book's end as a main character, evolving from hopeful idea to house to home."

—IAN MARSHALL, author of *Walden by Haiku* and *Story Line: Exploring the Literature of the Appalachian Trail*; editor of *Reading Shaver's Creek: Ecological Reflections from an Appalachian Forest*

"At the heart of this engaging biography of building a log cabin from raw trees is a couple daring to live the life they imagined for themselves. Ross skillfully includes the reader in this unconventional journey through writing that touches both the senses and the heart. She pragmatically explains the daily challenges of the project while at the same time nurturing a vision of living 'more connected to place, living lighter on the planet, and with more intent.' *The Log Cabin Years* is an excellent read for anyone searching for insight on how to build a more simple and sustainable life. What resonates most in this inspirational story, however, is recognizing the human capacity to accomplish the seemingly insurmountable—one step, or log, at a time."

—GRACE L. COGGIO, PhD, associate professor and sustainability fellow at University of Wisconsin-River Falls

"Creating a life as a married couple entails more than building a house together, or a log cabin in this case. But it's a good place to start as there might be no better way to get to know who you're planning to spend the rest of your life with than dealing with your partner's cranky exhaustion or annoyingly can-do optimism as you figure out how to get honest-to-god five-ton trees up the slope to the building site. While working a full-time job. And pregnant. Taking breaks only to do 2,000-mile hikes to remind yourself you can start big projects and see them through to the end. If this sounds daunting, it is. But the result—a magnificent, magical 2,500-square-foot home which is sturdy enough to withstand an earthquake and contain and nurture four creative lives—is worth it. I have a confession: the story made me cry. Not because Todd and Cindy occasionally brawled—I knew they would figure things out—but because it's a heroic story of a young couple taking a chance on a life that would be worth living for them, not a life that others prescribed. Cindy provides notes and tips at the end of each chapter, which are useful if you're inspired to build a log cabin yourself, but the real tips are in the story of how they found the will and the courage to be electrically alive on this planet."

—Bathsheba Monk, author of *Nude Walker*

"Reading *The Log Cabin Years* was an inspirational joy. Establishing their own interpretation of Helen and Scott Nearing's *Living The Good Life,* Cindy and Todd erected a living monument to their love and shared values. Their roots are strong; their soil is fertile; and the fruits of the magnificent tree they have planted and nourished over three decades represent a modern-day taste of sweet simplicity and healthy effort. The world needs their story now and I believe it will become a classic in the literature of sustainability—both physical and spiritual."

—Warren Doyle, PhD, founder/director, Appalachian Folk School

"In a world that is wrought with consumerism and materialistic lifestyles, *The Log Cabin Years* is a refreshing reminder that happiness can be found through our experiences and relationships with others rather than through money and power."

—Alicia Sprow, PhD, associate director for sustainable communities, Alvernia University

"Many dream of adventure. Some plan for and set out on adventures. A few even occasionally manage to have one. Then there's Cindy Ross—who *is* adventure. In her latest book—a housebuilding, marriage-making, child-rearing, life-living how-to—Ross shares the adventure in exquisite and revelatory detail. With high energy and deep spirit, she grabs our hands and invites us along. She insists we all hang out and hew a log or two (or twenty) before having a sweat in the sauna and hatching a new escapade: long-distance wilderness trekking with toddlers, anyone?"

—Maryalice Yakutchik, author and editor

"I have read several books about building log homes. *The Log Cabin Years* is more than just a how-to book on log-home building. Cindy Ross discusses in detail and with great sensitivity and humanity the range of emotions she and Todd experienced as they designed and built their log home on twelve wooded acres in rural Pennsylvania. Any individual or couple thinking about building their log home would be wise to consider the emotional aspects of such an undertaking and read *The Log Cabin Years* before they get started."

—DANIEL NELLIS, lifelong experiential educator and woodworker

Praise for
THE WORLD IS OUR CLASSROOM

"A love of the natural world and an understanding of our place in it are vital for humanity and all other life. Knowing we are part of nature and not outside it is vital for the future. The importance of this comes across strongly in *The World Is Our Classroom*. Ross taught it by doing rather than telling. Experience rather than theory. This is a book that shows just what is possible, a book that gives hope for the future."

—CHRIS TOWNSEND, award-winning author
of *Out There: A Voice from The Wild*

"School teachers are largely bound by classroom walls and the Internet; parents have no such constraints. As Cindy Ross reveals in *The World Is Our Classroom,* the unbounded opportunities in nature should inspire every parent to create memories and powerful experiential learning opportunities. Significant emotional encounters can be transformative. When children are allowed to explore, and use their curiosity to discover the seemingly magical things in nature, it changes them as no passive learning can. In this rapidly changing world, we must foster a love of nature in every child as they must soon confront profound ecological disruption and play a vital role in restoring, replenishing and relocating elements of biodiversity to retain some aspect of system integrity upon which all life depends."

—LARRY SCHWEIGER, author of *Last Chance: Preserving Life on Earth*

"Navigating the best educational options for your children can feel like you are lost amid a dense wilderness. *The World Is Our Classroom* cuts a path through that wilderness and gives the reader a map of how to teach their children the resilience, compassion, and problem solving that is part of adventure-based learning."

—JENNIFER PHARR DAVIS, author and National
Geographic Adventurer of the Year

"Cindy Ross is one of today's most eloquent and thoughtful writers on the connection between human and the natural world. *The World Is Our Classroom* shows how all of us invite humility and wonder into our lives, not only through great adventures, but through everyday communion with the rest of nature."
—RICHARD LOUV, author of *Vitamin N, The Nature Principle,* and *Last Child in the Woods: Saving Our Children from Nature-Deficit Disorder*

"We are encouraged to treat our children as if one tumble from the monkey bars or spiteful remark from a friend can cause a lifetime of pain. How exciting it is to see two parents put the world in front of their kids from such a young age, believing their kids will rise to the occasion. This book, *The World Is Our Classroom,* will explode some disabling myths about how fragile our kids are!"
—LENORE SKENAZY, founder of the book, blog, and movement Free-Range Kids

"In a culture increasingly alienated from nature and dependent on technology, Ms. Ross's book shows how our love for the world can be reanimated."
—AUDREY PETERMAN, president and co-founder of Earthwise Productions, Inc.

"Someone once said of Ginger Rogers: 'She does everything Fred Astaire does, but backwards and in high heels.' For me, that's what it's like watching Cindy Ross. She and I have both walked across countries, traveled all over the world, maintained freelance careers, and authored books. But in addition, Cindy and her husband Todd built their own log home with their own hands, and raised and schooled two children. Cindy's kids grew up with the world as their classroom. Want to live a big life? *The World Is Our Classroom* takes you on the journey of how one family did it, and it doesn't get any bigger, wilder, and better."
—KAREN BERGER, author of *Great Hiking Trails of the World* and the *New York Times*-bestselling *America's Great Hiking Trails*

"Cindy and her husband Todd have succeeded in accomplishing one of life's noblest goals—'to make one's avocation, one's vocation, as our two eyes see as one.' They have exhibited the courage, fortitude, and just plain old hard work, to create a life they fervently believe in and then effectively sharing it with their two children. The message in this book carries the truth born from actual experience. Read it, think about it, feel it, and then get on with making, rather than earning, a life for yourself and your loved ones."
—Warren Doyle, PhD, 36,000-miler and founder of the
Appalachian Long Distance Hikers Association &
the Appalachian Folk School

"Whether tightrope-walking a fogged-in Knife's Edge, ascending through the mist of Half Dome, or traversing slopes in grizzly country, Cindy and Todd present their children with breathtaking experiences that instill a sense of wonder, creativity, resilience, and self-confidence. The mental health benefits and lifelong lessons that come from extended time in nature resound through the book. Read this book before your children get sucked into the video-game vortex."
—Leo Walker, president and co-founder
of HIKE for Mental Health

The World Is Our Classroom is an enthralling education in itself for anyone eager to intimately experience the mysteries of the natural world. Cindy Ross has given us a treasure of environmental consciousness, empathy, and gratitude for the life we share on this Earth."
—Gail D. Storey, author of *I Promise Not to Suffer: A Fool for Love Hikes the Pacific Crest Trail,* winner of the National Outdoor Book Award

"Cindy raised her family with a real consciousness of the value of being in nature and adventure. Cindy and her husband Todd have shown that getting kids outside early makes them better people in the long run and it makes us better parents. *The World Is Our Classroom* is not about completely flipping your life upside down but making the time to take you and your children outdoors. It's a lot easier to hand your child an iPad instead of going on a hike but it is ultimately much more fulfilling."

—Corey Rich, film director and adventure photographer, author of *My Favorite Places—Great Athletes in the Great Outdoors*

"*The World Is Our Classroom* is a fascinating discourse on creativity and learning. This book will help parents find ways to nurture creativity in their children—particularly by taking them into stimulating nature and giving them the freedom to explore and wonder. In these pages, parents will come to understand how necessary it is to spend lots of quality time with their children. Building a strong and effective hands-on relationship between parents and their children is the best way to minimize negative effects from challenges such as drug use."

—Michael Kessler, acclaimed contemporary artist

"Schooling, too often, is a world where teachers and schools are encouraged with 'drill and kill' methods. This development of a new culture of schooling in America seems to mean that 'successful' students must learn to operate their digital apparatuses and attach themselves to their computer screens, or else risk failure. The online computer-based testing begs the question about which priorities are most important; test taking on a computer screen or true learning from experience and adventure as advocated for by Cindy Ross's book, *The World Is Our Classroom*? Cindy's belief in experiential education for her children, in teaching children to have sense of place, belief in 'The Nature Principle,' and having great adventures is well worth contemplating."

—Monty Thornburg, PhD, educator and president of the John Muir Geotourism Center

THE
LOG CABIN YEARS

ALSO BY CINDY ROSS

The World Is Our Classroom
Scraping Heaven
Kids in the Wild
A Hiker's Companion
Hiking: A Celebration of the Sport
Journey on the Crest
A Woman's Journey

THE LOG CABIN YEARS

HOW ONE COUPLE BUILT A HOME
FROM SCRATCH AND CREATED A LIFE

Written and illustrated by
CINDY ROSS

Skyhorse Publishing

Copyright © 2021 by Cindy Ross

All rights reserved. No part of this book may be reproduced in any manner without the express written consent of the publisher, except in the case of brief excerpts in critical reviews or articles. All inquiries should be addressed to Skyhorse Publishing, 307 West 36th Street, 11th Floor, New York, NY 10018.

Skyhorse Publishing books may be purchased in bulk at special discounts for sales promotion, corporate gifts, fund-raising, or educational purposes. Special editions can also be created to specifications. For details, contact the Special Sales Department, Skyhorse Publishing, 307 West 36th Street, 11th Floor, New York, NY 10018 or info@skyhorsepublishing.com.

Skyhorse® and Skyhorse Publishing® are registered trademarks of Skyhorse Publishing, Inc.®, a Delaware corporation.

Visit our website at www.skyhorsepublishing.com.

10 9 8 7 6 5 4 3 2 1

Library of Congress Cataloging-in-Publication Data is available on file.

Cover design by Erin Seaward-Hiatt
Cover photo credit: Cindy Ross

Print ISBN: 978-1-5107-6329-6
Ebook ISBN: 978-1-5107-6339-5

Printed in the United States of America

For Lila and Frank Fretz
Our mentors and very dear friends

Contents

Introduction   xvii

Chapter 1: Shaky Beginnings   3
Chapter 2: Groundwork   21
Chapter 3: Blockwork   33
Chapter 4: Setbacks   47
Chapter 5: Becoming   61
Chapter 6: Rainy Spring   72
Chapter 7: Dog Days   84
Chapter 8: The Big Wait   91
Chapter 9: The New Logs   103
Chapter 10: Another Hard Winter   123
Chapter 11: Help Arrives   135
Chapter 12: Full Time   144
Chapter 13: Orphaned   162
Chapter 14: The Trusses   168
Chapter 15: Separation   189
Chapter 16: Pregnant   206
Chapter 17: Grand Finale   222

Epilogue: 2020   238
Appendix: Log Home Building Basics   244
Glossary   251
Acknowledgments   258

Introduction

When we build, let us think that we are building forever. Let it not be for present delight, nor for present use alone. . . . Let it be such work that our descendants will thank us for. And let us think, as we lay log upon log, that a time is to come when those logs will be held sacred because our hands have touched them, and that men will say, as they look upon the labor and wrought substance of them, "See! This our Father's did for us!"

—John Ruskin

IN THE SUMMER OF 1978, I departed for the National Scenic Appalachian Trail (the AT) for Georgia with my sights set on reaching the summit of Maine's Mount Katahdin 2,100 miles later. When I finally stood atop that northern terminus of the AT, it was easy to believe that I could do anything if I wanted it badly enough. I felt that with passion and hard work, I could have any life I imagined. This was a monumental message for any person, but especially a young person who had their whole life ahead of them. This accomplishment had a profound impact on the adult that I was destined to become, and it has affected every decision I've made since. It happens to nearly everyone who thru-hikes a trail.

Three years later, I went on to hike the 2,600-mile National Scenic Pacific Crest Trail (the PCT). My hike was divided into two summers and the second year was spent with my husband, Todd Gladfelter, also a long-distance hiker. We spent many months living in the wilderness and were exceedingly happy.

On the AT and the PCT, we walked for many months, needing nothing to survive except for what we carried in our backpacks. Life was distilled down to the simple act of walking in profound beauty. Our bodies became amazingly strong and our heads clear. We saw that many of the material trappings of the modern world, which were absent out there in the woods, did not contribute to our happiness. Quite the opposite: acquiring things seemed to necessitate becoming enslaved to a process of generating more and more money to purchase and maintain them. As a result of this minimalist lifestyle, our needs in life became few and simple. We developed definitions of needs and wants that were very different from the rest of society. Freedom and independence, on the other hand, turned into requirements for our happiness.

Todd and I explored how we could design a minimalist, close-to-the-earth life after the trail. We looked for ways to incorporate those same ideals and principals we came to enjoy so completely in our trail life—ways that would give us the freedom to choose how we spent our time, to keep ourselves out of debt, to work at independent occupations, to create art, and to live close to nature.

We determined very early in our life together that we could either figure out a way to make more money or figure out a way to need less. By creating a lifestyle where only one full-time income could support both of us (thereby allowing us to work part-time with the remaining hours given to pursuing other interests), we could each have a manageable workload. We adopted this philosophy from Helen and Scott Nearing, authors of *Living the Good Life: How to Live Sanely and Simply in a Troubled World*, who were the de facto leaders of the back-to-the-land movement of the 1970s and 1980s.

As young people, Todd and I were no different from others who seek to discover what they like to do and who they are. We just chose an unconventional path. We designed a life where we were not buried under debt, we acquired skills that fostered independence, and we worked at occupations that gave us control of our time.

As a first step, we decided to look for land near the Appalachian Trail so that this important trail could remain in our lives as our family grew. We then decided to build our own home and learn to do every job in its creation ourselves. Todd wanted to learn as many homebuilding skills as he could and have that massive knowledge bank to invest in his adult life. He would take the lead and I would help as best I could.

Todd and I attended a ten-day log building school in northern Minnesota called the Great Lakes School of Log Building, where we learned the basics of log building. When we returned to Pennsylvania to begin to take steps to build our own home, we lived in a tiny rental bungalow (for fifty dollars a month) outside Kutztown, Pennsylvania, and then a house right in Eckville along the Appalachian Trail. The National Park Service, which oversees this long trail, had acquired it with a land parcel purchase. We were offered the opportunity to become "volunteers" in the park and manage a hostel for the long-distance hikers traveling through. Neither dwellings had plumbing nor central heating and there was no insulation in the walls. It was so cold in the park service house during the winter that the urine in my pee bucket froze overnight. But it was a sacrifice we made to save money, as we paid no rent. For seven years we gave up creature comforts for what we valued more: independence and freedom from debt.

The logs for our home were purchased from a local logger, and we taught ourselves how to do every job inside and out—from peeling the bark to scribing the logs to hoisting them in place using a skyline that we stretched between two large oak trees. We learned to lay the block foundation, do the roofing and build a chimney. We did everything except dig the foundation, put in our driveway, and drill the well. All these skills Todd picked up from books and a helpful friend here and there. (This was during the 1980s—before the widespread Internet and the wealth of information available from YouTube videos.) He also made most of our handcrafted wooden furniture, as fine furniture making was the occupation that he was trained in. Except for the logs (which only cost $2,000 in total), we used a lot of salvage that we got from my uncle who had a demolition company. Out of over forty windows, only the skylights were bought new. The bricks in the chimney were street pavers that we recycled. The slate roof was taken from a building that was going to be demolished. The cost of our entire home (including those services contracted out) came to just $20,000. Accomplishing all these jobs ourselves, of course, saved us money, but they also bolstered our confidence. Before we knew it, we were living a more independent lifestyle, saving money and getting an education. This massive building project stretched four full years. Todd also worked a second job at a kitchen cabinet factory all but the last year.

We accomplished building our log home for two reasons. We wanted to create a handcrafted home that we designed ourselves, one where we could have total creative control. We wanted to do it our way and not the bank's way, without a thirty-year mortgage, so in order to retain our power, we had to do it without a loan. We did not think that we could be really free to live the life we imagined if there was debt hanging over our heads. We were fortunate that during this time period, we had no building code in the rural county of Pennsylvania that we were living in. We only had to conform to an electrical code, and to pass inspection.

Of course, everything is a compromise. Four years of hard physical labor during which Todd and I had to learn how to bully thousand-pound logs into place were not easy. In the thick of our work, my three siblings, who worked "traditional" jobs and lived more "traditional" lives, used to ask me if all the physical labor and sacrifice was worth it. It was easy for us to answer affirmatively, for seeing our dreams come true has always been a top priority for us. Having a stunning, one-of-a-kind home and no mortgage was definitely worth it.

In retrospect, building a log home with a partner involved many facets of human life. In addition to the overwhelming job of learning the mechanics of solid timber construction, Todd and I had to quickly learn new methods of communication, methods that not only enabled us to do such intensive work for four long years, but to happily stay by each other's sides through it all.

Our log building teacher told us that some couples who try to build a log home together lose their marriage in the process. It quickly became easy to see how that could happen. There were new kinds of stress, insurmountable problems, questions without answers, and no place to turn for help. We each saw entirely new dimensions in our personalities that we hadn't known existed previously, and we didn't know how to react to them initially. But we vowed to build this home together and hoped to build an amazing relationship in the process.

THE FIRST YEAR
1985

1
Shaky Beginnings

I PLACE MY HANDS ON my knees and hang my head between my legs, trying to stop the world from spinning and fading into blackness. Sweat drips off the tip of my nose. My blond braid sticks to my neck. Gnats and mosquitoes buzz around as the August heat envelops me. "Are you ready?" a voice asks. I look up to see the swaying image of my husband, timber carrier in hand, ready to pull another red pine log up the hill.

"I've got to take a break," I announce, and go over to a spot of shade and collapse. Logging in the dog days of summer: close to 100 degrees Fahrenheit and 80 percent humidity, wearing long pants and long-sleeve shirts—buttoned at the neck and cuffs to keep poison ivy oil off our skin, as the plant covers the forest floor and the hairy vine grows on every pine we handle.

Todd and I are clearing land for our future neighbors, Rob and Barb Mull, for a view for them and a log sauna for us—a practice building before we tackle the monstrous job of constructing our own log home. After a few minutes of rest, we walk down the roughed-out "road," through clipped briars and between stumps to the pile of logs Todd had previously cut into "manageable lengths." Manageable for whom? A team of oxen? We kick the pointed hooks of the timber carrier, a tool that resembles an antique ice hook with handles, into the scaly bark and yank on the sixteen-foot log. The hook digs in deeper as Todd and I pull up on the wooden handles. With straight rigid arms, we begin the drag up the hill. But the handle acts as a lever and because Todd is much stronger and faster than me, he forces his end forward and my end backward. "Hold it!" I yell and stop in my tracks. "We have to pull *together*!" His silent eyes stare at me, screaming frustration. Our heads feel ready to explode from the heat, and so do our tempers. What he needs is another strong man or a team of horses, not a far weaker, annoyed wife.

Luckily, it doesn't take long to figure out that there *has* to be a better and easier way. With seventy-five logs to clear in the woods, we put our heads together and come up with one. The next day Rob arrives on the logging scene with a hood from a Volkswagen Beetle that he talked a junk car dealer into giving him for free. His plan is to use

it as a skidding sled. We flip the hood upside down and punch a hole in the narrow end. We pull a chain through it with a skidding thong attached to one end. The other end hooks onto the bumper of Rob's old, step-side, red International truck. We place a log butt inside the inverted, curved hood, kick in the hooks and yell, "Take it slow!" The little truck's engine whines as Barb cautiously pushes the accelerator pedal to the floor and coaxes the log up the hill. In a few seconds, we see the hood approach two protruding stumps. Before we can scream, "Hold it!" we watch in amazement as the hood's flexible sides fold up to accommodate the narrow passage, then uncurl back into shape after it moves through the stumps. Cheers resound through the red pine forest as we celebrate overcoming the first challenge of this log building endeavor. Many more lie ahead.

Once the logging for our sauna is complete, the logs are delivered to our tiny, rental bungalow. This is the first of two properties that we will live in while building our home. Delivery is made via my Uncle Iggie's dump truck.

Uncle Iggie is my Sicilian uncle. He has a blacktopping and excavating business and also does demolition work. Uncle Iggie keeps me abreast of any available salvage in the buildings he demolishes. We gather not only building materials such as bricks, lumber, and a massive slate roof but also interior goodies as well: built-in hutches, antique lighting, beveled glass windows and doors, wood flooring, and on and on. We crowbar the goods out and store them in a rental cottage on a friend's property that is twice the square footage of the bungalow that we live in. Uncle Iggie always whispers that I am his favorite niece, but I hear my other siblings receive this same affectionate message. He has a fierce old-country sense of loyalty to his family and an endearing roughness that makes him *my* favorite uncle, especially with all the gifts he bears.

The next evening, we go out of our bungalow to our log pile by the driveway, excited to move the first log back to our construction site and begin our log sauna project. When we finally move up to our land into our completed log home years from now, this sauna will have to be relocated. In the meantime, it gives us a place to practice our new skills while we look for much larger trees suitable for a house, as well as a piece of land.

We kick in the timber carriers and try to yank the top log off the pile. It moves an inch. When I try to brace my foot and pull, I fly backward onto the ground as the timber carrier releases its bite, chipping off a hunk of bark. "Let's try the come-along," Todd suggests, but there are no available trees to attach it to. "How about using the truck to pull it?" I ask. But the driveway is too steep and covered with loose gravel and all the tires do is spin and smoke. I drift the truck back to get a runny and accidentally slam into the pile, denting the tailgate and jamming it into the log pile. Now we can't go forward or backward, and the very top log—our very first log—still hasn't budged from the pile.

We go into the bungalow, our hearts heavy and our eyes brimming with tears. We sit on the worn love seat and stare ahead, saying nothing. All we can hear are the honeybees buzzing in the wall by our heads. If they find the uninsulated hollow walls of our old bungalow a good home, I think, maybe we should be satisfied, too.

After a long moment of silence, Todd asks, "How are we ever going to build a huge log home and move forty-foot logs twenty-five feet into the air if we can't figure how to move one skinny, lousy sixteen-foot sauna log?" I say nothing. What is there to say? The immensity of the task is suddenly startling. And this is a *tiny* task compared to the tremendous problems we will be up against later. The reality of it all hits us like a sharp, stinging slap to the face. Where did we get this crazy idea that we two humans could build such a house? Who put this dream into our heads? I can trace mine back to tenth-grade English class and blame Sister Dolores for making us read Henry David Thoreau's *Walden*. His powerful message, "Live simply!" changed the course of my life. I began back then, to feel like a handmade house of trees was the only home for me.

For many years following, the only log cabins that entered my life came as gifts from friends and family: cabins embroidered on throw pillows, cabins silkscreened on ceramic trivets, cabins needlepointed on wall hangings: trinkets to hold me over until the real deal. Years later, I learned of a hands-on log building school in northern Minnesota through an article in one of my father's *Popular Mechanics* magazines. I tore out the pages, filed it under L for log in my file cabinet, and put the dream on hold. First, I needed to grow up. Then, I needed to find a partner.

I found Todd Gladfelter in Port Clinton, Pennsylvania, back in 1980 when he was thru-hiking the Appalachian Trail. I was in his boots the following year and after moving near the trail, would frequently pick up hikers and bring them home to administer trail magic like so many had done for me: a hot meal, a shower, laundered clothing.

Todd's dream of a log cabin home began on our first date a few years later. As we walked in the Pennsylvania woods one autumn day, kicking leaves and sharing dreams, I proudly announced, "I'm going to build my own log cabin," to which he enthusiastically replied, "I'll help you." Looking at his six-foot frame with wide shoulders and strong arms, I believed that he could. I took him up on the promise. We got married in 1983. I was twenty-seven years old; Todd was twenty-three. We immediately began to plan how to turn our log cabin dream into reality.

I reach over on the sofa and take his hand. "We'll figure it out, honey. No one ever said it was going to be easy, but that doesn't mean we can't do it." He manages to turn his mouth up into a half smile, but his dark, sullen eyes shadowed by their long lashes tell me he's not convinced.

We've never done things the easy way in our short, young lives. When we wanted to experience the mountains of eastern America, we walked through the woods and over the summits from Georgia to Maine on the Appalachian Trail, carrying everything we needed on our backs in a backpack. We went into town every week or so to resupply, get a shower and a big meal, and then we'd be on our way. When we wanted to get to know our western mountains, we backpacked from Mexico to Canada across the Sierra and the Cascades for more than 2,600 miles. People told us it would have been easier and faster to go by car, but the experiences we had along the way could never be rivaled. For similar reasons, log kit homes were not for us. We wanted something a little more challenging, a little more original. We wanted to draw up our own design and plan, stay out of debt, learn skills, and create a home that exists nowhere else on earth. The Great Lakes School of Log Building appealed to us—a hands-on, intensive course where for ten days we learned the best way we could: by actually participating in building a solid timber log home.

After mailing in our registration form, we sent for logging and woodworking catalogs and pored over features of tools and prices. Weekends found us at antique markets talking with dealers and examining their tools.

The UPS man brought strange-shaped boxes with long handles sticking out their ends. After weeks of delivery, his curiosity got the best of him, and my deliveryman asked, "What's in here?"

"Pickaroons, peaveys, pike poles, adzes, slicks, and log dogs," we informed him, his question still not answered. It was Greek to us then, too.

A prerequisite for attending log building school was to read Canadian Allen Mackie's book, *Building with Logs*, considered the bible of log building. Mackie and Ron Brodigan, our instructor, teach the Scandinavian scribed fit method of log construction. The log walls are grown by placing each new log above the existing wall with a gap of about two inches in between. An instrument called a scribe is used, with a metal point on one end and an indelible pencil secured in the other. It opens like a draftsman's compass. A plumb and level bubble are mounted on it. As you trace the curves and bumps of the upper log, while holding the bubbles steady, they are drawn on the log below. The scribe is run down both sides of the log and around the areas to be notched. Once the upper log is rolled over, a groove is cut in it, following those lines precisely. The wood is then removed to create a flyway so that when it is rolled back into place on top of the lower log, it fits like a glove. There is no mortar chinking in a Scandinavian scribed fit

log home, no gap or airspace. The logs are worked green so as the house dries, shrinks, and settles, the joined logs tighten all the more. This method is more time consuming and requires more skill than other forms of log construction, but it is considered by many to be superior.

Part of what Todd and I quickly learn that first day on the sauna log pile is that although our teacher may have most of the answers, we couldn't possibly anticipate, in ten short days, all the questions that might arise. The log house on which we worked at school was at one stage of its construction. Steps like the foundation and the roof system had to be covered on the blackboard. As we are discovering, every individual situation has its own unique problems. Although Ron discussed various methods of moving logs at school, we primarily used a crane or the combined strength of sixteen able-bodied students. Todd and I are all we have to build our house. We have to rely on our imagination and ingenuity to make up the difference.

Another thing we have to remember is not to overwhelm ourselves with the monumental end result—a finished log home. It is enough to learn how to pull out this one individual log today. Our strength will build, as well as our tool kit of methods to move weight as the months and years of building go by. It is important, in times like this, to draw on our past life experiences and wisdom. I tell Todd, "We never would have gotten to Maine if we let all 2,100 miles of the journey overwhelm us at the very start. We climbed one mountain at a time, put our miles in each day, and before long, reached Mount Katahdin in Maine. Just as we reached the monument at the Canadian border on the Pacific Crest Trail. Let's tackle today's challenge: moving our first sauna log. That is enough."

When a situation looks hopeless and all energy, physical and creative, is devoured by that one defeating thought, "We can't do this," the only thing left is to distance yourself from the problem. Todd and I pull out the log building books onto the patchwork floor of carpet samples we tacked down for a rug. We stay up late, paging through books until Todd finally finds an illustration of a two-wheel contraption for transporting timbers.

The next day he fetches the snow tires that we kept when I totaled my old Datsun pickup in a car accident. In a chunk of oak log, he makes an axle for the tires, a little wider than our widest diameter log, and carves a notch in it for the log to sit in. The log, when positioned and balanced on the wheels, rolls easily by hand to the building site. But the problem of removing the top log from the pile and onto the wheels still remains. With his refreshed mind, Todd is able to see beyond our problem to a big tree across our blacktopped road (which wasn't obvious in his distressed and clouded vison the day before). He fastens one end of a rope to the top log and the other across the road to the tree. He puts me on traffic duty to stop cars, and easily come-alongs the log off the pile and onto the wheels. The system works perfectly. We get over the first mountain, but we begin to realize that a Himalayan mountain range lies before us.

Some people think we are foolish for taking the time to build this log sauna. The way Todd and I figure, we are going to make building mistakes, maybe even big ones. Why not perfect our skills on a small project that's not as overwhelming as a 2,500-square-foot home, nor as crucial? We don't have our house logs to begin building, but when the opportunity arose to get these smaller logs from our neighbor's land, we thought it wise to practice our recently learned log building skills.

The Great Lakes School of Log Building is located deep in the wilderness of northern Minnesota. There is no plumbing, electricity, nor central heat. Bathing is done the traditional Finnish way, in the dry heat of a log sauna—community style. In Finland they often sauna with family and friends, a tradition much like that of breaking bread together. The sauna room, kept pitch black for privacy and comfort, is heated by a woodstove. Cedar benches line the walls on two levels. The 200-degree, dry, penetrating heat relaxes every muscle in your body; the cold outdoor shower or plunge in the lake revitalizes every nerve. Going back and forth from heat to cold time and again gives you an incredibly healthy and relaxed feeling. After our first bath at log building school, all the students agreed that a sauna should be their first log building project. Finns build their saunas before they build their homes so they have a place to bathe and relax after a hard day of physical labor on their log house. It makes perfect sense to us, and it certainly seems more worth our time and energy than a log garden shed or an outhouse!

Ron Brodigan is the master log building instructor at the Great Lakes School of Log Building, which he started in 1975. He studied with Allan Mackie, the father of modern log home construction, and was a guest teacher at the Mackie School in 1983.

Ron possesses all the necessary skills plus more to make a chainsaw do magic. He demonstrates chainsaw techniques like brushing, feathering, and carving, that to us rookie firewood cutters, seem impossible. With a formal education in anthropology, Ron not only understands human beings intimately, but possesses the necessary communication skills to be a stellar teacher. In the 1960s and 1970s, Ron was a professional wood and metal sculptor, which is evident in his attention to detail and his craftsmanship. While he instructs, I write down nearly every word, draw diagrams, ask tons of questions, and shoot hundreds of photographs. Minnesota is a long way to go for help, and we don't expect a conventional building contractor back home will be able to give us one sentence of advice. I gather information at log building school like a squirrel gathering nuts. Todd watches intently and practices diligently. We each have our jobs at school as we do in every aspect of our relationship.

We practice, learn, and leave, buoyed by the knowledge that our fellow students, who had come from all parts of the country with the same dream, were now back in their states starting their dream just like us. This gives us confidence as we stumble through each step of the building process back home on our own.

Back home at our sauna building site, we select our logs, cut them to length, and raise them off the ground on skids. The next step is removing the knots and bark. We straddle the log, bend over, and pull heavy antique drawknives toward us, catching the bark and stripping it off. Sticky sap sprays my face and mats the hairs on my bare upper thighs. When we think of the seventy-five fourteen-foot logs we must peel to build the sauna and the three hundred twenty-five footers for the house, we realize it's a job we'd like to become friends with. After peeling three logs however, the pain in my lower back argues otherwise, and I retreat to a sawed-off stump in the shade to read through my notebooks.

I read Todd step-by-step instructions on how to cut his first notch. Before long, our first logs—our sill logs or base logs—are notched into place and the walls of our sauna begin to rise. The walls grow taller as we execute a few major tasks: the logs are scribed, the groove and notch are carved with a chainsaw, and then hand tools are used to clean it out and finish the log smoothly and exactly. The two most important steps

are scribing and sawing. I easily fall into the job of scribing, maybe from so many years of holding a paintbrush steady as I created paintings. With Todd's strength and strong back, both essential to long hours of extensive sawing, the bulk of the cutting becomes his job. If I draw the line incorrectly, it doesn't matter how precisely he cuts. If my line is perfect but he can't cut well, the log fits poorly and needs to be redone. On the rare occasion that a log doesn't fit perfectly, Todd has a "built-in safeguard," he says in jest. He can take his indelible pencil and draw another line on the edge of the groove, after he sloppily cuts the right one off and puts the blame on me!

Friends come periodically to help with the building. They are curious to see how it is done and entertain the idea of starting their own log project. All are men. Either they feel totally incompetent and fear they'll create more work from their mistakes, in which case they just peel (which thrills me), or they want to get their macho hands on that saw and try to make it dance like Todd can. After all, they've "been cutting firewood for years." The two techniques, however, are really opposites. In firewood cutting, downward pressure is applied to the chainsaw bar where the cutting teeth of the chain move around. In log building, you suspend the bar's weight and touch the teeth down gently only where you want the wood removed. Of course, they can't skillfully carve a notch without a lot of practice, so the next attractive job they want to try is scribing. After having to redo our friends' sloppy scribing by rolling the log over four times to correct the damage, that job, too, is removed from the list of helper opportunities.

When we consider the time it takes to teach our visitors, the energy we put out to correct their mistakes, only to have them usually never return, Todd and I realize we are better off doing those important jobs ourselves. Log building sounds glamorous, but it is difficult, skilled work and sometimes dangerous work. It can't be learned in a day, and progress is very slow. This frustrates many of our helper friends, as instant gratification has become a way for younger folk to measure an experience's value and worth. They expect to see the equivalent of an Amish barn raising occur, and if major progress isn't made, they often lose interest. More patience and perseverance are necessary to see the log building through than most folks possess. Living in our fast-paced world where things are done quickly and results wanted immediately, building a log home like this is even more challenging.

Every evening, after Todd's job as a furniture maker is over for the day, we go out to our front lawn by the little creek that sings past our bungalow and work on our log sauna. Summer rolls into fall and the walls grow slowly, almost unnoticeably. Progress on our primary goal, however, finding land, securing house logs and building a home, is almost nonexistent. Finally, we discover a piece of land on top of a low-lying ridge, next to our friend's property, Rob and Barb Mull, where we logged for our sauna. The land sends out feelers to us the very first day we walk on it; it feels like home. Soon after, my very ill father comes with my grandmother to check it out. He walks on it right before his lung cancer travels to his heart and confines him to bed. That day, when my eighty-two-year-old grandmother helps her son walk through the forest of ferns with his cane and her support, I know we will come to live there. Todd and I looked at other pieces of land that Dad never saw. It was one of the last times he walked, and I feel his spirit is part of these woods.

While we're in the process of having the land surveyed and purchased, we learn about a nearby spruce plantation in our county that is owned by the US Forestry Department that is being cut and harvested. Large, straight softwoods are rare in these parts of eastern Pennsylvania. Virtually none are cut for lumber. Instead, they are chipped and trucked to paper mills. If we want the logs, we have to move fast. Winter is advancing and the logger is ready to move into that area and begin cutting. People feel we are foolish for acquiring logs before we actually own land, but our landlord at the bungalow has given us permission to store them.

We travel out to the neighboring county where the forest is being cut to have our first experience with a logger—old Dory Angst, with his long, white whiskers, no doubt waiting for his Saturday bath and shave. His skidder, a machine used for dragging logs, looks like it moonlights in a demolition derby. It can't possibly be highway safe. Sure enough, no plates are on it. It gets hauled from job to job on a flatbed. We walk the forest tract with Dory, measuring the tree's diameters, looking for taper, straightness, and absence of branches. We tell Dory how wide we want them at the butt and how long we want them. He agrees to sell them to us at pulpwood prices, by the ton. We leave, hoping he will do what we ask. Those trees are not just raw material to us. They are going to be our home, our haven of security away from the rest of the world, a place in which to raise our children, grow old, make memories, and perhaps die.

It rains and gets muddy and Dory can't work. His truck breaks down and he can't work. His logger gets hurt and he can't work. He gets another tract to cut and he pulls out of our tract for a while. In the meantime, the sap starts to flow. This means heavier logs (from the weight of the rising sap), and more money for Dory, once he sells them to us, as we pay by the ton. It means more sap to sit in as we peel, more fungus and mildew will grow, and more insect infestation will occur. We are sweating it. On the day the logs are supposed to arrive, I sit on the interstate exchange and wait to lead the haulers through the complex maze of winding country roads to our landlord's meadow. Tears

fill my eyes as I run up to the truck and introduce myself to the hauler and blurt out, "Our home! You're bringing our home!"

"I guess if you have a good imagination, ma'am," the driver says.

HINTS & TIPS:

- When we began our homebuilding project, we were young and had limited experience, although Todd had been working as a woodworker and felt comfortable with tools. You could begin your cabin-building project using only books and videos for resources, while also enlisting the help of any family and friends who might be more skilled than you. Attending building school, however, or enrolling in workshops, can increase your skill level exponentially. You will learn about specific tools, have the ability to ask questions in person, and learn how to move heavy timbers, logs, etc., which is a huge source of challenge and struggle. Besides building skills, you will also learn a lot about your level of passion and your ability to see a

large log building project through and may need to realistically scale back your cabin's size, etc.
- Offer to help on someone's construction project to acquire a variety of skills and develop the necessary way to think in terms of building. That appreciative person may reciprocate when it's time for you to build.
- Shop for tools at antique markets and catalogs and begin gathering in advance of construction as acquiring tools sometimes takes time.
- Purchasing a very good professional chainsaw with enough power is essential. No homeowner model will hold up to the job. Having two saws is advisable. One should have a sixteen-inch bar unless the logs are larger in diameter. Have a file on hand to sharpen and an extra chain on hand to swap out.
- After over forty years, Ron Brodigan has retired and has ceased operating the fantastic Great Lakes School of Log Building. Ron has taught thousands of skilled log homeowner-builders and some professional log builders in the many decades he has been instructing. He has made his tool list as well as other important information available in this book for the future log cabin builders who read it.

THE SECOND YEAR
1986

2

Groundwork

ONCE SPRING ARRIVES, MY BELOVED father, who has been struggling for half a year with cancer, sadly departs this world. In the middle of our grief and loss, we are gifted two major blessings. We finalize our land deal and we learn of a vacant house owned by the National Park Service right on the Appalachian Trail that is in dire need of caretakers. Located five miles from our newly purchased land, it is the ideal spot in which to live while we build our home in the valley. This means moving our logs for the house and our not-quite-finished sauna to the new site. We hire the same men to haul the logs, spending twice as much money moving them as we did buying them. Over the winter months, the sauna logs dried to the point where Todd and I can carry a sixteen-footer in our arms with no problem. A Scandinavian scribed fit log house does not require spiking with tight metal pins to hold the logs in place. Instead, loose-fitting wooden pegs are hammered into drilled holes to prevent shifting, making it possible to unroll and move the whole building. We unroll the twelve-by-sixteen-foot building and load it onto the truck in an hour.

In June 1986, we walk onto our land for the first time, ready to scratch the forest floor and begin to build our house. We pick a level spot on top of a hill that is fairly open and sunny with only small trees and saplings to clear. It is most important for the house to face south to incorporate solar gain and be positioned between two massive oak trees that we will later need as part of a rigging system to raise and lower logs and position them onto our building. We whisper silent thanks to the trees as we cut them down, thanking them for the space and their use to warm our house someday as firewood. We cut sixty small trees in all, hauling branches to enormous piles to dry and later burn. We find peace in the hard work and feel connected to America's early homesteaders who cleared the land and carved a life from the soil.

This is why a log home is so appealing to us. We love trees. Our log home will look like the trees that once stood in the forest. As Allen Mackie said, "No stripped, chipped, cooked, treated, compressed, or otherwise manufactured product of industry can give such an awareness of each living tree just as it once stood." Bulging knots will remain, the carving lines of bark beetles will be preserved, unlike the machine-milled telephone poles of kit homes. As if all these processes are an improvement and nature isn't quite good enough. All the integrity, beauty, and natural protection will remain in the log and its spirit laid to rest in our walls. Todd tells people, "I don't want to build and live in a two-by-four-framed 'gorilla cage' home. Why saw a tree all up into small pieces, only to nail it back together again?" Our whole philosophy of living permeates our beings and makes the menial task of sawing trees and clearing land almost magical and certainly full of purpose.

Before we can begin the actual construction on our home, a preliminary step is to deal with our township's sewage engineer. A septic permit is required before a building permit can be authorized. The drain field must be located, the soil tested, and the system designed before house construction begins. We have heard horror stories about our area's sewage engineer—his lack of integrity, of his taking bribes and changing test results for a sneaky hundred-dollar bill; stories of making a landowner fill up his well with concrete because it was ninety-nine feet from his septic field and not a hundred.

When our prove pit is dug, it reveals clay two feet down—not good at all for a drainage field. Clay bonds the soil and does not allow liquid to permeate. Since Todd is working during the day, it is my privilege to deal with all of these procedures and work with professionals like our sewage enforcer.

When he comes to read our pit, I reach out my hand to shake and he will not even make eye contact. His gruff voice and red face match his heavy-set large frame. "It's no good," he tells me from his position down in the pit. "You'll have to put in a sand mound."

"We don't want a sand mound," I tell him, "They fill up in ten years, look unsightly, and are astronomical in cost. There has to be an alternative."

"*Get down in this hole, young lady!*" he orders me. "I want to show you what clay looks like." As I climb into the pit, I wonder, "Would he be talking to Todd this way?" Yellow-orange clay appears two feet down amongst the hairy roots of saplings. I assure him that I never doubted the clay's existence. There just has to be an alternative. He finally admits that we can put renovating fill on top, add another couple of feet of good draining soil, let it settle for four years and test it again for its water percolation rate. Maybe it will then pass for a standard system.

"We could also put in a composting toilet that takes no water," I tell him, but he knows nothing about them and doesn't want to learn, already convinced they don't work. When he asks what kind of house we are going to build and I tell him log, he bellows, "You won't get the electric company to put power in a log house."

"Why not?" I question him.

"Because they won't." he answers. Evidently this man has some sort of divine knowledge he's not willing to share.

He goes on to say that if we ever want the maintenance and plowing of our half mile of shale drive taken over by the township, it will need to be asphalted. He advises us to put $40,000 into a fund which he will hold for us in the event that it ever comes to that. "Then the money will be there," he says. I am speechless! How naive does this man think I am? We part company, not the best of friends.

It takes weeks to get more information out of him about the alternative fill and months more until we get our refund since we paid for a full perc test, which, I point out to him, he never ran. I spend hours on the phone with soil scientists learning about what kind of soil to use, how dry it should be, how large of an area to spread it on, etc. No prospective homeowner ever chooses this septic plan alternative because they don't want to wait four years before moving in. But that amount of time seems just right for me and Todd to build this house.

We finally get the okay to try the experiment and secure our building permit (ten dollars) already dreading working with this sewage engineer years down the road. It's good there are some jobs that aren't feasible for Todd and me to do ourselves, like installing our septic system, building our lane, pushing over stumps, and digging out our basement. There's nothing like bringing in a big machine to make it look like progress is being made.

Todd and I lay out the perimeter of our house with white lines of powdered lime. The hole needs to be seven feet deep and the rectangular sunspace we have planned needs to be five feet deep. We hammer stakes in the ground so Paul German, our excavator, can take depth readings from below in the pit. The dimensions of our house evolved while at log building school. Part of our curriculum was to draw up house plans in the evening hours and then transfer them to the classroom blackboard so our teacher, Ron Brodigan and the other students, could find drawbacks and make new suggestions. Our house dimensions were originally a twenty-five-by-forty-foot rectangle. But it was pointed out that forty-foot logs with little taper would be next to impossible to find in our part of the country, let alone be incredibly difficult to maneuver. By putting two jogs in our house we are able to use smaller logs without losing square footage and as well as add interest and variety. Since we don't want to deal with two jogs in our roof, however, we'll place a sunroom on one side and a porch on the other, thereby filling in the rectangle. This way the roof will have one continuous ridgeline and cover an unbroken rectangle of space. The blackboard session proved invaluable.

The only "blueprint" we possess to build our house is the pencil diagram we drew up on graph paper at log building school. In no time at all, the pencil lines fade and the scotch tape that holds the small sheets of paper together yellows, dries out, and falls apart. Since we are not expecting to need any money for a mortgage, we chuckle when we think of what a bank would say if we went in with our "plans" and asked for a loan!

The beauty of building a log home is the builder's—and the log's—ability to adapt to changes in plan. You want a window in the wall where one wasn't originally planned? Simply pull the chainsaw cord, for there are no nails or spikes to interfere. We presently know *only* the dimensions of our home's perimeter. How high it will be, where windows and interior studded walls will go, even how the roof will be constructed hasn't been figured out yet, nor does it need to be. With a log home like this, we can learn and figure as we progress. Conventional builders find this absolutely amazing. All we can do is grin when they ask who drew up our plans. Did we have an architect or had we sent away for them in a book? We don't show those battered and faded plans to many. They wouldn't believe we could actually do it . . . at least not until there's something wooden to prove it.

Before the hole for our home is excavated, we need to find the corners. We make batter boards—wooden stakes with horizontal cross members at right angles—and place them about five feet back from the actual corners of the house. Nails are placed on the cross members in line with the walls of the foundation. From the nails, strings are stretched from one corner to the next and where the strings intersect, are the corners of the house.

After the lime line is removed by the bulldozer, we need to find the corners once again, but this time, down below in the pit. Strings are re-stretched and from the intersections, a plumb bob is held, to find corners down below. The whole procedure takes forever. I never realized how precise and exact my husband could be until we get to this step. Once we find our corners, Todd pulls out his 100-foot tape and measures diagonals. When each diagonal equals the other to an eighth of an inch, he beams. When he's off by more, he becomes disturbed. Since it takes a while to build confidence, each day we return, we repeat the same measurements over again. Todd is fearful some neighborhood kids may have come and tampered with the strings overnight.

I am his tape holder. I stand quietly while he takes measurement after measurement. It's a tad difficult for me to handle sometimes, this passive role. My mind drifts to the book I'm writing, *Journey on the Crest*, about my hike from Mexico to Canada on the Pacific Crest Trail that needs more work. I think of all the other things I could be doing besides holding the end of a tape for hours.

So, I ask questions. That sets Todd into a frenzy . . . being questioned, especially when I ask him why he didn't write the number down the last time we measured it, instead of doing it again and again. Or I want to know exactly what we are doing and why, to break up the monotony. "I have no idea what I'm doing," he says. "And it's difficult enough without you making me feel like a jerk by asking me things that I don't know."

"We're partners," I remind him. "I have a brain, too. Maybe I can help you figure it out."

Later on, I ask one too many questions, and probably in a frustrated tone because I am really getting tired of waiting, waiting, waiting. "I'm going home!" he yells, this quiet, subdued husband of mine whom I've never heard raise his voice let alone argue. "I've had enough!"

"You are not!" I yell back. "That's not how you work out problems. What are you going to do when we have a problem over our child? Run away? Deal with it! Let's work it out!"

Todd is used to working alone and figuring things out inside his own head. When I want him to put his thinking into concrete words and sentences and share them with me, so I can understand, too, he can't seem to do it or doesn't want to, and I remain ignorant and frustrated. "I like to work alone best," he tells me.

"Too bad," I reply. "You're stuck working with me for the rest of your life." Todd also likes to do things for himself, anything and everything, especially if it saves money. I thought I knew the extent of this until I find him making log dogs. These are two-foot-long metal "staples" that are hammered into the logs to hold them in place while working. The dogs prevent the logs from rolling. Although they can be purchased for ten dollars apiece, Todd has decided to make his own from rebar. Todd's torch isn't quite hot enough to bend the metal, so he takes his hair dryer outside, sets it on "high" and shoots it through a tube to raise the temperature of the torch flame. It works!

I am not quite so amazed at his ingenuity and his desire to save money the next time. We have to build wooden forms to hold the poured cement that will become our footers—a thick, narrow "sidewalk" that the block basement wall will sit on. But he cannot get wooden stakes into the ground, which is near total shale. So, he decides to make his own stakes from rebar, which must be sawed to length with a hacksaw. "You're nuts!" I tell him. "It will cost five dollars at a weld shop and take five minutes. You will probably go through ten dollars worth of hacksaw blades and take all day." Todd leaves for work and I drive to Empire Wrecking in Reading where Shorty runs a used building supply warehouse.

"Hi beautiful!" says the short, white-haired man with the baseball hat, the words filtering through his giant, stinking stogie.

"Got any rebar, Shorty?" I ask.

"There's a whole pile over there. Help yourself," he tells me. I load up the truck with small pieces that are short enough to not even need cutting. "How much do I owe you, Shorty?"

"Nothing. You're looking mighty good today." In the reflection of my car window, I see what he's talking about. I had run out of clean T-shirts that morning and had thrown on my younger brother's outgrown hand-me-downs. It's just a trifle too small or "just right" as Shorty would say. Needless to say, when Todd comes home from work, he is overjoyed with the contents of the trunk and doesn't mind giving up that job after all, especially at that price.

We had heard lots of stories from people about pouring footers. Our excavator had advised us to have plenty of guys with wheelbarrows when the cement truck delivers "because you only have one hour to unload the truck. After that, you pay by the minute." Whoa! Our house perimeter is quite big, plus we need additional pads for pillars, a chimney, and the basement steps platform. We line up three more folks besides Todd and me to help.

We had also heard horror stories of flimsy wooden frames being pushed out by the pressure of the wet concrete, spreading it everywhere. Todd wants to make sure these forms are sturdy so that doesn't happen to us. The lumber we're using for our forms came from our carpenter friend, Joe Donmoyer, one of my past backpacking students when I taught adult education at a local community college. Joe had been working on the second floor of a wood frame building when it collapsed. He barely escaped in time as the building, the size of a football field, crashed to the ground. (It actually needed the support of metal beams.) Before his company could collect insurance, all $60,000 worth of lumber had to be burned. Unless it disappeared first.

The sturdy two-by-tens that Joe salvaged from the wrecked building are more than enough support for concrete forms, unless you're as fanatical about your forms as Todd. Against them, Todd sledgehammers his rebar stakes in everywhere, nailing on bracing and cross bracing every few feet. It looks as if he's building a fort, but he still has his doubts. He drives me crazy with his radical mood swings, one minute thinking it won't hold, and the next convinced that it will. "What else can we possibly do?" I ask in frustration that night over supper dishes.

The concrete man is stopping by to inspect the forms on his way home from another job. Todd waits by the telephone like a nervous teenager waiting for an answer for the prom. I can tell the outcome when I see his face light up in the receiver. First, he just listens. Then he says, "Well, I never did it before, I wanted to make sure I did a good job."

"What did he say?" I ask, when he hangs up the phone.

"He just kept repeating, 'Whoever built those forms did a helluva job!'"

"YEAH!" I shout and toss down my dish towel to throw my arms around him in a hug. "The footers are on the way!"

The big day arrives—the first concrete evidence that our house is taking form. Todd rolls over in bed and looks out the window. The sky is gray and the foliage damp. Concrete trucks don't pour in the rain. He rolls back over, depressed. "Call him," I say. "It's not raining yet." He gets up and goes downstairs and starts to putter, putting off the impending bad news. He empties the big water bucket under the sink that substitutes for plumbing, feeds the cats, and dumps the garbage out on the compost pile.

"Call him!" I plead again. "Don't be so sure he's not coming." He finally does, and the answer is "GO!"

We have three wheelbarrows and three friends who are giving up their time for free to help us: Frank Fretz, Mick Charowsky, and Dave Crosby. Half the area can be reached by the truck's chute, the other half must be wheeled over and dumped. I will be the raker. The guys will dump the concrete into the forms, and I will spread it out. Frank is in his mid-fifties and older than the rest, so he volunteers to be the "chute director" and "wheelbarrow filler." We all know our jobs and are ready and waiting for the truck to arrive. Only one hour! We can do it!

The mortar rushes down the chute, quickly filling up the wheelbarrows. In rapid succession, each man comes over and dumps his load. I rake like crazy until the next load arrives, fifteen seconds later. The wheelbarrow drivers need to be strong and swift. Drive it hard and dump it fast. If they take their time and cautiously tilt it into the

trough, they'll lose their momentum and dump it outside the forms. They dump, and I rake. Suddenly it seems like night has fallen. The sky darkens, thunder rocks the heavens, and rain pours down on us. My big, blue cotton T-shirt gets soaked and stretches below my hips. I wipe mortar off my cheek with my elbow. Still, we dump and rake and move like lightning.

"*Holy crow!*" the driver says. "You guys are going to break the record."

"How much time do we have?" I ask.

"Two more hours and fifteen minutes and you're almost done *now*."

"Our excavator told us we only had one hour to get the job done," I tell him.

"It's determined by the yard," he says. "Concrete is measured in yards. Your excavator probably had three or four yards in his job. You have *ten*, and a lot more time." We all laugh at having taken bad advice. What did we know?

We have a picnic prepared for our helpers, but the rain drives them home, all except Frank. We sit on our front porch back home, eating ham sandwiches, chips, cream-filled donuts, and shoofly pie, watching the storm roll out and feeling very satisfied. We toast with water and on our slate message board Frank writes in big, bold letters, "THE FOOTERS ARE IN!"

HINTS & TIPS:

- Ideally, it would be best not to be working full time while you are building your log cabin so you could concentrate on getting it built as quickly as possible and maintain the integrity of your logs, so the wood does not rot, mold, and become infested with insects.
- Study floor plans and seek ideas for every part of your building: decks, porches, roof systems, etc. Have your basic design already decided upon when acquiring logs so you know length and diameter needs. You may have to alter your design once you know more about the logs you will be able to acquire.
- The most efficient building shape is a square, which has the fewest number of walls. Since we desired a rectangular house, we made two squares, offset instead of one big rectangle. We had more notches to carve, but we were able to keep our logs more uniform in width and they were not as heavy to lift.
- Thirty years ago, the only building code our township had was an electrical code inspection. Our building permit was a mere ten dollars, and we could build anyway that we wished. Since 2006, all that has changed. All the permits necessary to build a home now cost about $1,000 in our area and half a dozen inspectors must be brought in to check out the individual stages of construction: the footers, the framing, the roof, the plumbing, the wiring, etc. Inquire about your township's rules and regulations beforehand so you are not caught unaware and can plan accordingly.

- Not every public servant is there to help and make your job easier. Educate yourself, be assertive yet respectful, but don't let them take advantage. You need to work with them in order to attain your ultimate dream of a log home, but that doesn't mean they can abuse you.

3

Blockwork

FIFTY-SEVEN-YEAR-OLD FRANK FRETZ HAS A personality like a little boy—playful, easily excited, and full of spirit. His slim frame and sandy-colored hair help him look years younger. He tucks his shirt into his underpants, and when his britches fall down in the back, a few inches of his brilliant white Fruit of the Looms peek out. He buzzes around the building site, happy to work and share his knowledge, grimacing as he crinkles up his nose in an attempt to hold his eyeglasses on his nose after they slide down, too busy with his hands to push them up. Frank is a very talented natural history illustrator, but today our friend is teaching us how to lay block. "I'm tired of drawing those dumb little flowers and birds," he teases. "I want to do something *fun*!"

Frank's father was a carpenter whom he helped on many projects while growing up, and like Todd, he loves manual work. It seems to be the Pennsylvania German way, a heritage both men share. He shows us how to mix mortar on our trays of recycled highway signs and washing machine sides. I mix and pat my mound of "mud," cut it into meatloaf-like slices, and gently plop it onto the block's sides . . . "buttering block." I'm setting Todd up to do his job. He'll grab my blocks and gently place them on the wall. Frank makes Todd lay the very first block and teaches him to build corners.

Todd is a fast learner. He soon has his favorite way of doing things, sometimes contrary to Frank's. Both men like to be bosses, both think their way is a trifle better, but both are good-natured and give each other room. After a few hours of laying, it feels as if we've worked with block for years. We were a little apprehensive about taking on this task when our carpenter friend Joe, who went to building school for three years, said he would *never* attempt such a project. Even the basic masonry books we studied told us to leave laying concrete block to the professionals. We wondered if we were being naive and foolish. No, we discovered.

This job requires skill, but nothing complicated that an untrained "handy" person can't learn. Todd defines a handyperson as someone who tries new things for himself, practices until he develops a sufficient amount of skill, and gains enough confidence to go on to the next project. I, myself, can say, "I know how to lay block." Not that I know everything there is to know about the job, but enough. This process of house building is beginning to feel like a metaphor for life to me. Frank's wife, Lila, fears my female children may feel inadequate trying to live up to their mother. I disagree. I hope my female and male children won't be afraid to try new things, whether they excel at them or not.

I'm not doing anything most women aren't capable of doing. I use my body. If you use your body over and over to do things, it gets strong, and you gain confidence. I don't believe that building a house has to be a "man's project." I'd never say I was equal in strength to Todd, but I do the best with what I've got. If women want to be independent and free, they might join more in the work traditionally reserved for men. It saddens me that there are so many women frightened of spreading their wings and trying new things, but it's a fact that basically no women come to help on the house.

All except Lila. She has been a wonderful example and mentor to me. She mixes mud to the best consistency—never too wet, never too dry. She had a lot of practice on the home she and Frank built themselves. They disassembled a post-and-beam carriage house and carried it, timber by individual timber, on the roof rack of their beat-up old station wagon, from sixty miles away. When they turned fifty, she gave her husband an ultimatum: "Either we hike the entire Appalachian Trail or we sell our home in the Philadelphia suburbs, build our own home, and raise our own food." Frank chose the latter and they fashioned a life much like that of Helen and Scott Nearing. These friends have been nothing but an inspiration since they came into our lives.

While we wait for them to arrive this Saturday morning, I mix a batch of mud, as usual, while Todd sets up. "What do you think?" I call him over to check on the mud. "Does it look okay?"

"Looks good to me," he replies. But it turns out to be much too wet. The sand got rained on last night and already has a large amount of moisture in it, before I add my usual amount of water. I don't know enough about mixing mud to take this into consideration. The blocks sink and Todd can't lay. He decides to wait awhile until it stiffens up. We stand around and watch it, spread it out to dry, and hoe it some more. He tries another block, and that sinks, too. I add some more dry ingredients, and it's still too wet. "Why don't I mix another batch and let this one sit?" I ask, but Todd is paranoid that he won't be able to work that fast and it will go to waste. "I'll just add more water if it dries out," I tell him, but he doesn't like that, either. His brow tightens and his dark eyes get stern as he walks away.

When Frank and Lila come, I tell them of our little problem and Frank simply comments, "That's no big deal, just mix another batch."

"Todd must learn to adjust," Lila says, "to more things than just mortar," and we laugh good-naturedly. Todd doesn't take too kindly to her comment, however, or to our finding amusement in his lack of adjustment. Before long, the second batch is used up, and the first batch dries out enough so we're able to lay with it.

The next day Todd mixes a batch of mortar while I set up. When I go over to fill a bucket with mud, he smiles at me sheepishly, "It's too wet," he says. He adds more sand and mortar mix. "It's still too wet," he says. I just smile and say, "It's not that easy mixing perfect mud, is it?"

In these first months of house building, I can see my shy, introverted husband changing already. He loves laying block, loves seeing progress on the house. When he gets stuck, he calls Frank. Frank can

usually solve anything. If he doesn't know the answer, he'll look it up in a book or creatively think of or design a solution. It took some work to get Todd to go to Frank. Todd doesn't like to bother Frank and feels that he ought to be able to solve his problems on his own. But when our half dozen books don't possess the needed information, he has no place left to turn.

Before, Todd only felt comfortable talking to people about backpacking and hiking, his first loves. He needed to have something strongly in common before casual conversation felt comfortable. But so many men are drawn to this house-building project, men who may have the same dream themselves, men of all different ages, from all walks of life. Todd is so proud, and the conversation flows easily, like never before.

Todd recently changed his shift at the Quaker Maid Kitchen Cabinet factory to have plenty of daylight to build, even in the winter months ahead. As a result, he's home during the day and can make his business calls himself, order materials, etc. Up to this point, answering the phone was like forbidden territory. His own father avoids a ringing phone like the plague. When we first got married, I made sure I was always involved with something and unable to answer it, to get him used to making casual conversation. When he called about some building material, he'd ask, "Do you carry such and such? . . . Okay, thank you," and quickly hang up. I'd ask him: "What's the price? Are they in stock? How many? Can they be ordered? What are the store's hours?" He's making progress. This house building is going to be an amazing confidence-builder. In taking charge of this extraordinary project, my husband is taking charge of his life.

Frank says I look like a block layer: sleeveless, cutoff T-shirt, boots caked with mud and gray mortar dust. I *feel* like a block layer. I put up my string and begin laying my own line. I call Frank over occasionally, master block layer, and ask what I should do in a case like this.

Some of the men who come to help us know less than me. Todd avoids teaching or instructing as he's uncomfortable in that position, plus he's ultra-conscious of not making them feel uncomfortable, so the job falls on my shoulders if it needs to be done. Our builder friend Joe, who said he would never attempt such a project himself, is here offering his assistance. I work my own wall until the blocks reach three rounds high and are too difficult and painful for my back to pick up. I go over to help Joe, stay in the sidelines buttering block and setting him up. I'm not so sure how much he knows or what his personal way of doing things is, or how he feels about a woman giving him instruction on a building site, so I just observe covertly behind the stacked block. Todd and I have never had any issues about gender in our relationship, but I know that is not the case for all men.

Joe's wall is an inch lower than his string and he is smashing and smearing the mortar joints all over the block's sides. I have to look at this basement wall a long time after our friends leave, so I casually give him pointers when I see him becoming dissatisfied with his results. "Frank showed me how to scrape the mortar this way," I say. Joe is incredibly humble. Frank stops over and says, "Let the inch go. Make up for it on the next round."

"Block isn't my forte'," Joe says. But I answer, "This is a good way to learn. Try again." The next row comes out beautifully and he enjoys the rest of the afternoon so much that he doesn't want to leave when dusk settles.

Before departing for the day, Frank and Todd take transit readings on the halfway-finished wall. Todd is off only an inch from one wall to the other. He is elated. Joe whispers to me, "I can't believe how fanatical he is. It isn't necessary." But it is necessary to Todd. It's his way of doing things, and it can only make the next step easier. Frank and Todd quickly measure diagonals before going home and find they are *feet* off, not inches. Todd and Frank stand there in disbelief, at opposite ends of the tape, panicking. Lila yells from the back of the pickup she's loading, "Check it again! When something is that far off, your figuring is wrong!" They stand there baffled, quietly searching their minds for an explanation. I watch as they go through the motions again measuring one rectangle, and then the next. "You're going from outside corner to outside corner and inside corner to inside corner," I say. It hits Todd like a bolt of lightning. Frank still doesn't see it, and I try to explain. "Never mind," he laughs embarrassed. Later, I explain on paper on the faded hood of our truck, and the third time he grasps it, feeling sheepish.

It's very interesting to observe our male helpers on the work site, on what has traditionally been known as their turf. Frank became embarrassed when his building mistake's solution was discovered by me, a woman. Joe felt inadequate when he didn't do as good a job at laying block as me, a woman. We're all learning side by side. We're all problem solving as we go, men and women alike. Women tend to ask questions

right from the start, and do not pretend to know more than we do. The men will ask each other, but it takes a lot for them to ask advice from their wife. I feel as if I am furthering my education about men through this building project. I learned boatloads about men when I was only twenty-one and worked in underground iron ore mine.

Back in 1975, the labor board told Bethlehem Steel's Grace Mine in Morgantown, Pennsylvania, that they had to hire a certain quota of minorities and women to work in their underground iron ore mine . . . perfect timing for me—a young woman with a burning desire to be a professional artist, looking for some big money to go to art school. Underground mining was considered a very dangerous occupation, so we got paid handsomely to descend into the bowels of the earth.

At first, women in the mine were not openly accepted by the male miners. Since the mine was newly established, most of the employees had recently walked a different path. Former farmers and farriers now drove eight-yard-wide scoops, learned to drill a blast pattern and blow up the drift face with tubes of nitroglycerin. Back home, their wives baked pies and canned sauerkraut. In the eyes of these men, women didn't belong underground. I had to earn their respect. Ours was an interesting ratio: eight hundred men, twelve women. I needed a crash course in assertiveness training.

In the first few months of employment, we women were "muckers," shoveling heavy, wet iron ore from underneath the mobile belts that carried the raw material out to the shaft. The muck dropped off the conveyors, built up underneath and prevented movement. Our job was to get the belts going and keep them going. We handful of young women built muscle mass and learned if we had what it takes to work underground with a group of manly men.

In time I came to love the mine work—the challenge, the new skills I was learning, my developing strength, and the men themselves, as they came to accept me and became my friend. At the end of that year, I had hundreds of "uncles" and "cousins" and a few boyfriends who took me hunting and fishing and motorcycle riding. Reading books on assertiveness training helped me find my voice. I believe it's this "men's work" and "women's work" distinction that messes things up. Putting women on the building site begins to change all that. And it should, in the long run, help us both in our journey to become whole.

Jean Brogley is short and built like a football player. He carries his arms away from his barrel chest because they're too big and bulky to hang straight down. An ironworker from Pittsburgh, he climbs twenty-story steel frameworks and cuts and welds in the sky. We attended college together years ago, and I haven't seen him since. He called on a whim, wanting to visit for the weekend, so he is here helping us lay block.

Except for a little less hair that's revealed when he lifts his Steeler's baseball cap to wipe his brow, he looks exactly the same. Although we don't have many things to talk about, working side by side in an old friend's company is a treat in and of itself. Because he is recovering from a back injury, I butter all his block and set him up to prevent him from needing to twist.

Our mortar today is being mixed by Uncle Sam's twin, Chuck Wood. His long, curly, strawberry blond hair frames his bearded face with an American-flag bandanna tied around his neck. But this man isn't stern with pointed fingers. He has the jolliest disposition and keeps us all in stitches with his stories and jokes. We share a history of being thru-hikers on the Appalachian Trail. He, too, is recuperating from an injured back and has just recently gotten out of traction in the hospital. He mixes mud while concentrating on keeping his back straight.

Quiet, shy Steve Ambler, also a long-distance, Appalachian Trail hiker friend, works as hard as the rest. He talks so softly it sounds as if he's mumbling to himself, but he's really just saying he's not happy with his work. In spite of his apprehension, he's doing a fine job, like all the rest. These folks are neither family, nor very close friends, yet they're working hard for us, for our dream. I believe they are curious about our home-building project and interested in learning and so they are willing to sacrifice their time. Todd and I are deeply touched by their help, for their presence and joyful attitudes make the job fun. And we desperately need to finish the basement in the next weeks, for the electric company has given us a deadline for laying our foundation. They will indeed bring electricity to our log home, contrary to what our sewage enforcer said. They even drew up a plan for their lines where they put them on the border of our property, as well as a few of our future neighbors. It enables us to attain electricity for free for what would have cost $10,000 had we been requesting it solely for our own home. The electric company needs some kind of concrete guarantee that the customer is indeed serious about building a home before they run the lines, so they want our basement finished before they begin. It's late October and with the help of this weekend's work party, we shouldn't have any problem meeting that deadline.

Because of the big push to get the job done quickly, I'm afraid I've injured myself. After buttering block all day long and not rotating jobs, my right wrist has started to ache. For ten long hours, I twisted and turned my wrist, a mortar-laden trowel in my hand. Whenever friends come to help and bust their butts for us, Todd and I feel we must work just as hard, if not harder along with them. Today, the pain is intense, but thinking of our friend's sore backs, I cannot say a word about my wrist and continue using it.

The next day, Monday, I can barely move my hand. The simple task of washing dishes, sloshing a dishrag back and forth, produces excruciating pain. How much good can a crippled hand do when it comes to daily chores, let alone building a basement? All the tasks are now dumped on Todd.

I take some time off to heal. In a week, I go up to the land and try it again. Only my left hand, the uninjured one, is functional for scraping joints and striking, but before long that wrist begins to ache too from its unaccustomed workload. I'm feeling like I'm not much good to have around, and Todd continues to absorb most of the jobs.

Today is windowsill #1 day. Tomorrow is windowsill #2, etc. Todd's goal is one windowsill a day. He takes so much time smoothing out the concrete and making it perfect, you'd think he was being graded on it. When he tries to slip the aluminum window frame between the block, it is way too tight. Someone advised him to make the opening "snug," although Todd was thinking it needed room for expansion. Disgusted with himself for not listening to his own mind, he forcefully tries shaving down the metal with his woodworking plane. Still it doesn't fit. He threatens to chip out the concrete block and destroy the corner, so I suggest taking the window home to grind it smaller. But according to Todd's schedule, the windowsill is supposed to go in today, not tomorrow. When he looks at the strapless watch he carries in his pocket, he discovers that there is very little time left before he must pack up for

home so he can go to work—his "paying" job. All the mortar must be used up NOW!

"Take four sheets of paper," he instructs me, "and make a ball out of them." I am to stuff them in the holes of the top blocks so he can fill them up with mortar. I take four sheets and roll them into a ball. Todd looks at me and repeats, "I said, take four sheets and roll them into a ball." Am I being dense? Isn't that what I just did? I go through the same procedure which is still wrong. His voice rises and his very expressive eyes fill with anger, "Maybe you should have stayed home. I can get things done a lot better by myself."

This shocks me and shuts me up. Here I am risking my health with an injured hand which may be stopping me from illustrating my book and writing, and he doesn't appreciate it. I finally realize that he wants four balls from *each* of the four sheets of paper.

After I roll his precious balls I pack up the truck noisily while avoiding all eye contact, so he knows that I am not happy with him. I walk out to our gate and stand with the cable and the lock, ready to close it when he drives through. Then I notice that my engagement bracelet is missing from my wrist—my thick, silver, Navajo bracelet with the beautiful turquoise stone and the heartfelt, engraved message from my fiancé. It's lying on the ground on top of my flannel shirt back at the site. When I walk back, he's standing there with it in his hand. I try not to look at him but I do anyway and he's smiling—highly unusual for him to snap out of his sour mood so quickly.

"What are you going to do with him?" he asks me. I say nothing. "He seems to have a problem working with other people," he says about himself.

"That is a real problem," I remark, "since you aren't building this house alone."

"I like things done my way," he goes on, "It's usually a better, more efficient way of doing it."

"Other people have good ideas, too. You must learn to delegate jobs with patience and understanding and give specific instructions if you're so fanatically picky. Besides, where's this husband I used to know who had a confidence problem? You act downright cocky. Sometimes I think I'd rather have him back!"

After three weeks, my wrist heals completely and Todd and I finish the basement walls. We build pillars to support the interior log walls and call the electric company with the good news that the job is complete, which is great, because it's getting late. It's mid-November and the season is changing.

For a solid week, it rains every day, and Todd becomes very ill. He comes home from work feeling achy and stiff with such a terrible headache that it prevents him from moving at all. When three days go by without any improvement, I scour the home medicine journals worried about the possibility of spinal meningitis. I inform him, "One more week and you're going to the doctor."

"Doctor" is a dirty word to Todd. So is "pill." He fights the smallest aspirin and even an occasional vitamin. When the rain stops, he suddenly announces that he is miraculously and completely better and ready to go back to work.

When we arrive at the site, we walk toward the basement wall with the same anxiety we experience when we top a snowy mountain pass on a high-altitude trail. What will we find on the other side? What we find in our basement is water—a foot of water, like a swimming pool. With the end of the rain came the entrance of a cold front. Todd scrapes the ice off the wooden ramp leading down to the basement floor with a flat shovel. He crouches low as he scuffs down the ramp, so that if he falls, he'll be closer to the ground. Water rushes over the tops of his rubber boots and fills them as he steps off the ramp. The ground beneath the water is hardened and compacted from our constant walking and mortar spills. It allows little or no water to drain into the earth.

Todd fills two five-gallon plastic buckets and attempts to walk up the icy ramp but slips and goes backward. "This isn't smart!" I say. He comes out and we look the situation over and begin to consider alternatives.

If water is allowed to lie in there and freeze, it will push out our block walls. (The excavator told us about a crack he once saw in a wall that was so wide you could put your arm through it!) Should we buy a pump? Buy a generator to run it? Should we dig a drainage ditch? Should we just try to empty it out with buckets every time it happens this winter? Maybe we should try to cover it for the winter? Buy huge tarps? But there's nothing to support them. They will just fill up with rain, droop, and become like a lined swimming pool of water. Should we try to get a subfloor down? This would entail a huge amount of work: putting down our first logs, our main beam, and all of our log floor joists, which must be flattened by hand and notched in. It could never happen in the next month before the dangerous freezing weather starts in. We cannot easily run these questions by our log building teacher, Ron Brodigan. Ron only has a radio phone in that Minnesota wilderness that he accesses infrequently, so Todd and I have to make our own building decisions.

The freezing morning air and these unanswered questions make me shiver. Once again, that overwhelming, helpless feeling rushes over us. We climb into our red pickup truck and drive home in silence. Once inside, Todd stretches out on the floor, four inches from the orange glow of the kerosene heater, with his coat, boots, and hat still on, and slowly announces, "I think I'm getting sick again."

HINTS & TIPS:

- If your mind tends to think in 3D as opposed to 2D, consider making a model to scale, much like Lincoln Logs. Todd's model enabled him to visually see where he needed cross logs for support, where windows should be located, where he could incorporate shorter logs, etc. Having a model made it handy for Todd to reference it throughout the four years of building.
- If your log cabin will sit on a huge woodlot and you have considerable trees to harvest, you should consider investing the money into a bandsaw mill. You could flatten your floor joists and create your own dimensional lumber if you were interested in doing your own logging.
- Don't be afraid to try new jobs that you have never done before. Most skills can be learned and result in at least an acceptable level of success. Reach out to friends and family to learn who already has experience and who amongst them might be willing to share their knowledge. If you can't find a way to pay them back personally, assure them that you will pay it forward when someone asks for your assistance on a project. Each one teach one.

4
Setbacks

It's December and it's cold and it's very difficult for me to get excited about working outside. The big push to complete the basement forced me to abandon my other interests in life as well as my work—writing and painting. I'm starting to feel deprived. I have these feelings of not caring so much about the house. It seems like such an obsession with Todd. I know it's my house, too, and that I should be putting in equal time. I want this dream, but I have other dreams and needs that aren't being satisfied and fulfilled. Baby time is rolling closer with every passing month and year, and I'm not getting any younger nor getting any closer to accomplishing what I want as an artist-writer. Lila says I seem tired lately. My body doesn't feel fatigued, but my psyche does. I reread my journal and find it peppered with worries and frustrations. My earlier journals, written before I was married and before I began to build a log house, contain such carefree enthusiasm, but I was still unsatisfied without a man. Now that I've found him, and such a good husband at that, I can't understand my problem.

Todd's mood always affects mine, whether I want it to or not. It can't be easy for him, having the primary responsibility of building this house. It's probably quite frustrating for a talented furniture maker like Todd to spend so many hours a day working on an assembly line in a kitchen cabinet factory. He is doing it for the money, because the pay is excellent, and we need the money for building materials. Todd works the second shift, from three until eleven, in order to take advantage of the precious daylight to build our home. He tells people that log building is so hard that he goes to work "to rest," and he is *still* the fastest, most conscientious worker on his shift.

We've been shoveling dirt and rocks for the last two days. Our excavator presented the brilliant idea of dumping some excavated dirt into the basement to level off the floor and protect the footers from frost and thereby save money on purchasing stones. It sounded good to us. But when we tried to spread the first huge pile, our metal shovel points sank in two inches before hitting resistance, large rocks glued together with hard wet clay. We had no choice but to pick it apart with pickaxes! Today the temperature is so low that the dirt piles are frozen solid, so we can only peel logs. We enjoy the warmth our bodies are putting out from the exertion but soon realize that the sap and moisture in the logs have frozen, making the job twice as difficult. My drawknife takes only little bites, and they are an effort. Todd takes hungry, gulping bites with his, attacking the log and taking the bark off in long strips. The guys from the electric company are up here this morning, putting in our power, so I go over to chat, rest my weary arms, and watch them auger holes into the earth to set poles. I admire their one-piece insulated suits because already the cold has crept in and is making me shiver. "I'd like to get my husband a suit," I tell them.

"You should get yourself one, too," they say. "You're out here working. Better yet, forget your husband. You're colder than he is. Just get yourself one." For some reason, I wasn't even considering a suit for myself, not being the primary log builder, but they are correct. I matter just as much.

After a while the line workers come over to check out our building project. They ask a few questions about our method of joining the logs and when I say the word "chainsaw," one replies, "Oh, that's cheating!"

I think to myself, *cheating?* Peeling three hundred logs by hand, and they're telling us we are cheating.

"They didn't use a chainsaw years ago," one remarks.

"This *isn't* years ago!" I reply. What a strange reaction, this "cheating" business, and this is not the first time we've encountered this attitude.

After the men leave, Todd needs help rolling a log. When it's done, I say, "What can I do?"

"Hone the drawknives. Take the knots down on the floor joists. Go level the basement."

"I can't take the knots down because my saw is too dull," I reply.

"Sharpen it."

"I don't know how."

"Learn. I have to sharpen and maintain all the saws. I have to do *everything*."

I take off my leather gloves in this frigid weather and angrily rotate the oiled stone in a circular motion to sharpen the drawknives. My bare fingers are getting colder and stiffer by the minute. I don't know if the line worker's comments made him angry and he's taking it out on me or what. I finish, return to Todd and say, "I would have taken the knots down with my dull saw, but the logs are too heavy for me to turn without your help."

"Then learn to move them yourself."

All I wanted him to do was to set me up so I could work and not have to stand around idly and freeze, but he didn't want to stop what he was doing, which is always of paramount importance.

"Bring something to draw then," is his next sarcastic suggestion.

"It's fifteen degrees! My fingers couldn't hold a pen."

Actually, I'm glad that he's expressing himself. He used to hold all of his anger in, look at me with dagger eyes, but never say a word. How that used to break my heart when we were first married. I'd much rather share his frustration and the cause of his anger than be subjected to crippling silence.

I catch a softening in his expressive, dark eyes, a sparkle. Even without his mouth transforming into a smile, I can see his mood change. But I try to be tough. It's so difficult for me to stay mad. I'm a firm believer in blowing off steam. Soon he's telling me that he loves me. I look at him crooked with dirty looks.

"You don't have to love me now, that's okay, but I love you." How can I resist those warm, puppy-dog eyes? We smile and hug. He does get all the shit jobs—the most strenuous and difficult ones. Whenever there is a choice between two jobs, Todd always lets me choose. Invariably, I pick the easier one. It's not that I'm slothful, I just tire quicker and my back isn't that strong. From time to time, Todd naturally resents his work overload.

"It's our anniversary today, you know it, pal?" I inform him, "And we're fighting!" We decide to quit work immediately, have Todd call in sick at his job, go to the grocery store, and buy expensive food for dinner.

"I'll pump water and heat it on the stove to wash up," Todd offers. "We can unplug the phone, nestle on the sofa, and read old love letters from before we were married." Sounds great to me!

Our house is frigid when we arrive home after working all day. Our antique cookstove's firebox is small and the wood burns out in two hours. After lighting newspaper and kindling, we jitterbug around the living room floor—fully clothed in outdoor garments, warmed by the exercise and each other's love.

At supper I comment, "Can you imagine going out to the gym to work out and get in shape? It seems so absurd. The women at Wyomissing Institute of Fine Arts asked how I stay in shape." (I do part-time modeling for life drawing class and art students.) "I didn't know what to say at first. Then I laughed and said, 'We live hard. We pump our water, carry firewood, mix mortar, lay block, peel logs. We don't have to work out to stay in shape, we just live our lives and it takes care of itself.'"

Todd finds it confusing when people buy riding lawn mowers to take the work out of the job but then spend large amounts of time in indoor gyms, pushing metal around, toning flabby muscles they no longer use. His philosophy is if he walks behind his mower, he has more time in the long run and gets fit besides. This house-building project is making more than one part of Todd and me strong. Every obstacle we overcome, every fight we come through still holding hands, builds strength—the most important kind of strength . . . love for each other and the ability to keep on trying.

Just because we have fights doesn't mean we care less for one another, but in our case, probably more. We feel more secure in our relationship and don't fear each other's rejection if we need to express our frustration. The amount of stress that accompanies this sort of project for novices like us is extraordinary. Todd doesn't do well under pressure, so he is also learning how to deal with that besides teaching himself new skills. He knows he often snaps at me, which is a real change from the way he was before. I tease him when he behaves like this, but I am grateful for the change. He knows I care what is going on inside of him and that I want him to share it.

And of course, I never hesitate to share my feelings with him. On this cold December night, I am feeling like hell. Not only does my body ache all over, but I also have a cough that has lasted for days. My cough from a cold probably turned into bronchitis, but I've been trying to ignore it.

Today, Todd and I shovel stones from the outside, down into the basement hole. We each take a shovel and fling the scoopfuls over our shoulders. When the huge pile disappears up top, we go down into the pit, spread it around using a wheelbarrow, and rake the floor flat. Next comes spreading hay around the concrete footers to insulate it from the cold and prevent them from heaving up when the thermostat drops low this winter. We bought inexpensive spoiled hay from a mushroom farmer that was rained on too many times and got moldy, so it couldn't be used for growing mushrooms. It is matted and wet and often difficult to pull apart. Clouds of white moldy powder, like lime dust, fill my lungs as I tear the bale apart with my fingers. I turn my head to avoid breathing in the worst. But within moments, I begin to cough uncontrollably.

Tonight, at home, I cannot stop coughing—a hoarse, dry cough that hurts my chest and lungs. It was five degrees outside today while we worked, and this evening, it is not much above forty degrees *inside* our house. Getting up to urinate in the middle of the night takes unbelievable amounts of energy, I am so weak. Come morning, Todd gets up, begins dressing, looks at me lying in bed and asks, jokingly, "Aren't you getting up today?" In all honesty I reply, "I don't believe that I can." He sets me up in bed with hot tea and toast, pills, the tissue box, and a book and drags the kerosene heater up the steps to warm the room. Time crawls all day.

The next day I am able to stand up. Making progress. But Todd comes home from work feeling ill himself. He's often tired as soon as he wakes up in the morning, which is when you're supposed to feel most refreshed. I wonder how he gets through his shift, for he's usually ready for bed when it's time to leave for work in the middle of the afternoon.

What are we doing to ourselves? We don't seem to know when to stop. We slow down and rest for a spell when we feel ill but jump right back into the work soon afterward. When we're fighting off sickness, it also doesn't help to live in a house like ours that is so cold so often. This National Park Service house that we live in has no insulation or plumbing. This tract of land was purchased through eminent domain when the Appalachian Trail was moved off the road. Buildings are usually dismantled that are attached to a purchased parcel, so manning the house is a first for the managers of the AT. Todd and I get to live here for free as caretakers, but part of our responsibility is running a free shelter-like hostel for the thru-hikers on their way to Maine in one of the outbuildings, but the house also came "as is"—as in no plumbing or running water, no central heat, and no insulation. Todd and I haven't stopped working long enough on our log house to buy plastic and staple it to these rickety windows, so the breeze coming down off the mountain blows right through the house. During the winter, it's so cold that my pee bucket freezes overnight. We heat water to do dishes and immerse our hands in the basin just for the warmth. "My God, this feels good. Can you imagine what a whole tub of bathwater would feel like?" It is not a good house to fight off illness when your resistance is low.

A friend is coming to help us today. I'm not feeling strong, so I decide not to go over to the land. Todd doesn't know if he can handle working, either. Soon I hear him running up and down and up and down the steps at full speed. "What are you doing?" I ask. "Exerting," he answers. "If I can exert here and not feel like I'm going to die, I should be okay at the land."

At dinner, I can barely speak. My voice cracks and disappears. Laughing sends me into fits of uncontrollable coughing. Something is very wrong with me. I spend most of that night sitting up in bed hacking. The coughing is so violent it makes my head, back, and chest ache. Next morning, a Sunday, we find ourselves in an urgent care clinic. I have pneumonia.

Recovery is very slow. Lifting my arms over my head makes me tired. Sitting at a table makes me tired. Walking across the street to the outhouse totally wipes me out. I feel like I'm recovering from a major operation. I can't imagine ever being strong again.

Christmas comes and goes and the New Year, too. My antibiotic pills are almost gone, which should mean I am better, and Todd would like to go up to the land and work. May as well see if I am strong enough. I dress warmly, putting on long underwear and lots of layers. My job on the building site is to fluff up the hay in the basement with a pitchfork. After three or four forkfuls I am drained and the white, moldy powder sends me into the truck cab in a coughing fit. I sip almond tea, hold the plastic thermos cup in my bare hands for its warmth. I let the steam cover my face and fog the truck's windows while trying to calm down and stop the coughing.

I stay in the truck until Todd needs me, when he can no longer progress in his work without assistance. I roll on out of the cab, help him muscle a log onto the building, and quickly return to the long vinyl seat of the truck to lie down and recuperate. Building this house feels so urgent; a race to get it up and roofed before the logs rot and get devoured by bugs, a race to complete it so we can start our family, as I am not getting any younger and I absolutely must wait until the heavy lifting is finished. And so, sick or not, I at least try to help Todd when he needs me so one of us can keep working.

That night, a major snowstorm hits, making it impossible for us to get up our half mile-long shale driveway to build, let alone push

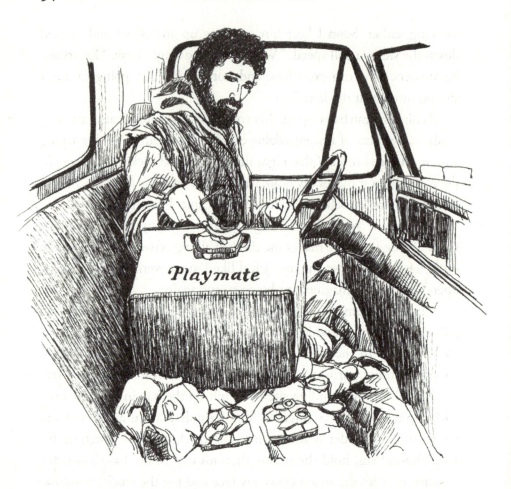

logs around on our wheel carrier. Since winter's cold has settled in, we both resolve to shift our sights away from the building and on to other things (like getting well for starters!). There is no more discussion about how to cover the footers to protect them or pressure to have a certain amount of work accomplished before winter sets in. It has arrived.

Now we can take a break from the building. Now I can stay indoors and rest and recuperate and do some of the other things I've been neglecting in my life. Todd, too, can become strong and fight off catching my germs, as we so often pass them to each other. I set my sights on illustrating my Pacific Crest book—weeks of doing fine line drawings under the warmth of a high-intensity lamp. Todd concentrates on completing our sauna—work he can easily do himself without my assistance.

Since we began work on our land last June and all through the block laying this past fall, we have not only worked on our house but have also tried to pick away at finishing our sauna—two major construction jobs. Progress on both has been slow. Now, Todd can concentrate on the sauna. Windows are built and installed. A door is crafted and hung. The floor is laid, the roof is on, and benches inside and out are built. Todd buys a fifty-gallon metal barrel and makes a woodstove out of it, which for safety purposes, will be fed from the outside of the sauna. All that remains are the rocks needed to heat the room and radiate warmth. The rock needs to endure extreme heat and not splinter and shatter on the sauna takers. Calling around, I find there are two sources of igneous rocks to purchase: one is across the country in Seattle at fifty dollars for ten pounds; the other is across the ocean in the Scandinavian countries for an even saltier price. We could use a couple of hundred pounds to do a good job. People give us all sorts of ludicrous suggestions, not the least of which is surrounding the stove with old cast iron baseboard heaters and old engine blocks, but we aren't pleased with those choices aesthetically. A few hours north of here, however, marks the edge of the glacial remains from the last Ice Age. Perhaps we can find some granite along the Delaware River, a rock that is second in line to fire-formed igneous for saunas.

On a cold, rainy March morning, equipped with raincoats, high rubber boots and buckets, we stop at nearby Hawk Mountain Sanctuary to purchase a book on Pennsylvania's geology to aid us in our search. Jim Brett, the curator, calls a geologist friend to give us some last-minute tips for finding river rocks. He instructs us, instead, to look for a rock called diabase, which we've never heard of. "Diabase would be better than granite. There are a few intrusions in the state where the metamorphic rock was pushed up," he says. Todd and I have no idea where to look for this rock or what it is we are even looking for. Just then, another naturalist, Tom Lecky, yells in from the other room, overhearing our phone conversation. "I have diabase in my garden. I've been digging the rocks out for years and have nice little walls of it built around the garden. You can have all you like!"

All right! We pile in our truck and drive to his home an hour away. We fill the truck's bed with five hundred pounds of the ruddy looking diabase. But the truly amazing thing is our friend lives in a tiny village called Finland! We take a picture of our truck full of rocks on the town square, with the local restaurant, the Finland Inn, and the Finnish flag waving in the background! Now we can say, we went all the way to Finland for our sauna rocks!

Todd and I make up invitations for our first sauna party for all those who helped on the project. I make a banquet of Finnish and Scandinavian food and announce to everyone, "The Finnish sauna is finished!"

When we began building last summer, I decided to keep a journal of what we learned and how everything transpired. I was hopeful that Todd would contribute, too, so that his words and feelings, his voice, could be heard and understood. After some encouragement, reluctant as always to reveal his thoughts, he writes:

> I stand back from the sauna after putting the last screw on the gingerbread fascia. It's done! It's a beautiful, solid looking building. I'm smiling and filled with pride. I think of all the hours we worked on this building, while everyone said we should have invested them in the actual house. But I know I did it the best way. If the house had come first, it may have been too overwhelming. At times, I wondered if I would ever make the roof of the sauna. But after going through the whole procedure once, I have no doubt that I will also reach the roof of the house. Mistakes were made on the sauna that can be avoided on the house. Less strength will be wasted, work will be more accurate, along with the accepted knowledge that it

is slow work. More progress can be made by avoiding wasted energy instead of pursuing a hurried pace. The sauna was a confidence builder and my skills were honed. I now know I am a log builder.

HINTS & TIPS:

- Safety is of the utmost importance. Wear Kevlar chaps, at least (see appendix) whenever your saw is running. Steel-toed boots or even total Kevlar boots are a good idea in case you drop a log on your feet, as well as protective eyewear and hearing protectors. (A chainsaw shirt is also available.) A comprehensive tool sheet can be found at the end of the book, provided by Ron Brodigan of the Great Lakes School of Log Building.
- Depending on where you live and the climate, cut logs will not last forever without getting rotten or buggy. Try to be efficient and use your cut logs up within a year. If your construction project is going to span years, and you'll need multiple loads, plan to spread out acquiring your loads of logs.
- Building a log home can be a huge project. Focus on the job at hand. Don't allow the enormity of the project to overwhelm you. Take one step at a time. Learn one skill at a time.

THE THIRD YEAR
1987

5

Becoming

Spring is in the softened air, geese are flying overhead, warmth summons life from the ground, and I am anxious to be on with our dream. "Let's build!" I say to Todd excitedly, but tools go into the truck slowly. Todd looks annoyed as he mutters under his breath about the length of time it takes to load the truck and then unload the truck. I close my ears to him, safeguarding my joyful mood.

At the site, Todd walks around the perimeter of the wall, checking for cracks in the block. When he comes around to the front, he stands there, arms hanging straight at his sides, not moving at all, while his eyes go from the trees that are too close to the building and need to come down, to the dead branches dangling from their trunks, to the firewood pile that collapsed over the winter. "I don't know where to start," he says, looking very disturbed and distressed.

"Let all that go," I say. "Let's put a log up."

He moves in slow motion. "I have no energy, no motivation," he admits.

"That's okay," I answer, "I'll give it to you. I have enough for both of us." We go out to the log pile to bring a log back.

"Where does it go?" he asks, "I think we need to measure it," and stands there frozen, not knowing what to do next, as though he's never done it before.

"Your tape is on your belt, like always," I help him out. The log is extremely difficult to put on the wheels, for Todd cannot remember

how to position it. Anger suddenly fills him, and he picks up the heavy log singlehandedly without warning me nor telling me to move away and throws it onto the wheels.

"Okay," I say. "You're not being smart now. You're going to hurt yourself or me. What's the matter with you, don't you feel well? Do you have a health problem or a mental problem?" I badger him. He delivers that famous Gladfelter response, "I don't know."

Todd's body is very much connected to his mind. When he's overwhelmed and stressed, it makes him feel and perhaps actually become physically ill. It's difficult to tell which comes first sometimes.

"You need to figure out why you're behaving this way so you can decide either to stay and work or go home. I can't tell what's happening inside your body." He stands there, trying to figure it out. I wonder if he's uncomfortable with starting to build again. Lately he seems to always have a reason for putting it off. If that is the case, he needs my encouragement. I ask one more time, "Do you think you're getting ill?"

"Maybe. I might be. I couldn't concentrate at work last night," he continues. "Instead of cutting my usual four hundred cabinet doors, I only cut a hundred. I seemed to work in slow motion, not being able to concentrate."

We both agree that this is no place for an unclear mind, so we pack up and go home. Once again, Todd finds his place next to the kerosene heater on the floor. At night, he sweats out whatever sickness he had in him with five visits back and forth from sauna to a cold shower. He's always been able to fight illness well. He can often lick it overnight with a good night's sleep. He'll kick himself in the butt the very next morning and will himself back to work. But if it's a stress-related illness, he only pushes it underground and it continues to come back and haunt him. In bed at night, as we hold hands and pray out loud. Todd says, "Dear God, make me a peaceful man."

"Honey, I didn't realize you had so much stress," I say.

"I want to cut firewood for next winter," Todd says, "turn over the garden, and spruce up that old chicken house for the twenty-four peeps we ordered."

"Something's gotta go," I announce. "The chickens! Let's cancel the chickens. That's one thing we can cut out to make more time." He likes the idea, too.

A week goes by and I let him do his other chores without uttering one word about my wanting to go over to the land. Hopefully, he'll catch up and once again find the passion to build. Come Saturday, the weather is gorgeous, and I am going stir crazy from being inside drawing. "Let's build!" I say. But the head log builder isn't enthusiastic. He draws back the heavy, sliding garage door and stares at the stacks of pine boards blocking the entrance that we purchased at a public sale this week. They were placed here temporarily and need to be moved. I know what he's thinking. He has to deal with the lumber before even considering building. Is he finding excuses, or does he really need such order?

"Leave it," I tell him. "Do it tomorrow when I'm at work."

"There isn't enough time to go over and build," he replies.

I silently count the hours of daylight left in the day. Six hours! "There's plenty of time! Let's do what we can. We have to get moving on this house!"

"I'm not in the mood!" he shouts.

"Too bad!" I shout back, losing my patience. He sends his precious antique, hand-forged chisels and chainsaws over the top of the wooden truck rack, crashing onto the metal bed with such force and carelessness I can hardly believe my eyes. This isn't like him. Something must really be wrong. He ordinarily shows the utmost respect for every one of his tools and cringes whenever someone lays one on the ground.

"I am sick of loading this truck!" he yells. "If you want to work so bad, YOU go over and put that log up yourself!"

"I can't," I reply. "I need you to help me. Look, I am really anxious to build. I have to work at the university quite a few days this week and this is one day I'm free to help you. All those other days when I am busy, you can do those things like stack lumber that you don't need me for."

"I don't need you to put that log up," he says uncaringly. "I can do it myself. I have so much to do and I don't know what is more important."

"*The house!*" I yell. "We've got to get that house built!" He storms away ranting and raving . . . unusually demonstrative behavior for him. We finally climb into the truck and begin our drive over the mountain, but he stares straight ahead, eyes fixed on the road as if we are driving through a blizzard or a dense fog. "I know how you feel, honey. I don't always feel like working, either," I tell him. "When we were logging in August, I certainly didn't want to go. But we have to, things need to get moving." I put my hand out, palm up, asking for his on top. At first, he looks at it and ignores it. I persist, holding it outstretched. Then he slips his large, muscular hand in mine and smiles faintly.

I don't believe in staying mad long. It eats up too much of your life. I used to give Todd a time limit—one hour to be angry. Now, he's pretty good at snapping out of a bad mood with only a little bit of encouragement, if a bad mood is what it is.

The log we must move back to the building today is the longest, thickest, and heaviest of the entire pile. We have much difficulty getting it onto the wheels. "How did we do this before?" I ask.

"I don't know," is his informative answer. On most days, I usually do what he tells me to do. But today, no words of instruction are coming out of his mouth. I finally figure it out myself and we proceed to pull the log down our shale driveway and back to the building. But the slightest uphill stops us in our tracks. We grunt and expend tremendous energy but never budge the log any further. The log is so long, its front end is dragging on the ground. No matter how low we drop our arms, we can't get the log to rise. One of the tires is also stuck on a little rock. We have to back the log down and try again. "Give it hell, honey," I say to Todd. "Let's hear some sound effects!" We take a long "runny" and push like hell to get it over the incline and thrust one end onto the building in one smooth motion. All right! Now the other end.

"A ramp! We should set up a ramp, right?" I ask the chief log builder.

"Okay," Todd answers, willing to go along with anything as long as he doesn't have to think. I run and get a board, and position it, but the log won't slide up the plank.

"This is crazy." Todd says. "We can't do this."

"Yes, we can!" I defy.

"Let's try to push it with our hands first," Todd suggests.

"*Wait!*" I yell, as we begin to pull up the low end of the log. "The end already up on the building could roll into the basement hole once we get this end up. Let's put a wedge under it." I run for a wooden wedge and jam it under the round log. We pull again, and the higher up the ramp the log gets, the harder it is to move until it, finally, will slide no more.

"I don't want to build anymore," Todd suddenly says. "I'm tired of all this." I ignore his comment totally. I'm still treating his behavior as a bad mood, not illness like the other day. *You need to be a mind reader with this man*, I think.

"How about trying a lever and a fulcrum, like the trail crews use to move heavy bridge logs?" I run and get a board and lever it onto the building. We look at each other and smile, give the thumbs-up sign, hammer two log dogs in, and go home. Three hours to put one log up on the building. With a third person on a weekend, the same job would take ten or fifteen minutes!

On the way home, I try to encourage Todd, "You don't become a master log builder overnight. We didn't start out knowing how to build the sauna, either. We have to take our time to figure things out. When it comes to sawing and scribing—laying down logs, we know what we're doing. Once we learn how to move these honkers, log building should go much easier." We have arrived at the place where something must be rigged up to help us move the logs.

The logs are just too heavy for our four arms alone. And this problem of Todd not wanting to build must be dealt with before any more progress can be made. Since I'm going out of state for a hiking club meeting without him this weekend, I feel it's a good time for some in-depth reflection and writing. I leave him the following letter with some blank sheets of paper for his reply.

My Dear Husband,

I need to understand why you are avoiding work on the house, why you are not happy about going over there. As your wife, I want to help you with your problems, but I need to know how you feel. You've never been taught to get in touch with your feelings and emotions, and this colossal project demands it. Please take some time thinking about this and come up with some answers. We'll talk when I return.

Love you, Cindy

As I drive down the interstate, my mind is a flurry of thoughts. Todd spends his days rushing. Rushing through meals, standing by the toaster to gulp down breakfast in order to get to the land and squeeze in a few hours of work before rushing back home. Then, I quickly prepare him a hot noonday meal, pack his lunch in half an hour, and push him out the door to go to his paying job. He returns after midnight, happy to finally collapse in bed, knowing he must get up the next morning and do the same thing again. How can Todd work a full-time job *and* build our log home, without becoming too fatigued with the entire endeavor, without becoming burned out and sick, without neglecting his basic need for sleep and a healthy diet, and somehow maintain a sense of humor through it all? It's too much to ask of him.

I compare this house-building goal with our long-distance quests on the trails. When we slogged through rain and cold for days on end and asked, "Why?" we learned it was for the greater goal, the greater good, for what we were "becoming" because of our toil. So, what exactly are we "becoming" through this project? Sure, a home is becoming, and a big, fat debt *isn't*. Our marriage is evolving. We are developing a lifestyle where there is *major* interdependence. Todd and I are together all day long, sharing nearly every aspect of our lives.

And what about me? I wonder about my own mental growth, where I am now. Am I going backward or forward? I used to spend so much time reading philosophical and metaphysical material, but all that "heavy stuff" becomes irrelevant when you're trying to build a log house. Why logs? Couldn't we have chosen an easier path?

"Develop character!" a voice yells from inside of me. Walking from Georgia to Maine and Mexico to Canada was supposed to accomplish that. "Growth is painful!" I yell back to the voice. Todd and I need to examine these questions together. We need answers to help guide and illuminate our path through these dark, foggy nights.

While Todd does some introspection of his own, I take the opportunity to learn more about the dynamics of our relationship from my good friend O. W. Lacy, Doctor of Psychology at Lancaster, Pennsylvania's Franklin & Marshall College. O.W. is an Appalachian Trail 2,000 Miler and he has been conducting an extensive study with the Myers-Briggs personality test and long-distance hikers. Todd and I were both tested in the past, and O.W. holds insightful knowledge to the inner workings of our separate personalities. As we share the ride to the hiking club meeting, O.W. sheds some light on what's happening.

On the Myers-Briggs indicator, Todd and I tested alike in all categories except one. Unlike myself, he is an introvert and learns by observing, watching, drawing conclusions inside his head from what information he picks up from the outside. I am an extrovert and communicate and exchange information verbally. When confronted with a problem, I figure things out by talking, discussing, or writing to bring order to my thoughts. I need to solve problems with contact, exchange. When Todd becomes upset, confused, or emotional, on the other hand, he internalizes his feelings and problems. The stronger his emotions, the less he is able to express himself or talk about it. During these times, he cannot think, and if forced to, becomes more emotionally disturbed. Therefore, when I push Todd to think or communicate when he is upset, he shuts down. He merely says, "I don't know," if he says anything at all. I can hardly believe that his mind becomes so incapacitated, so unable to function. I make matters worse by my exasperated, extroverted emotion, driving him further inward and making his mind even cloudier.

In my struggle to personally understand the problem at hand, I force Todd to go against *his* true nature. But when I try to subdue myself, try to remain quiet and give him time to feel these feelings out, think his thoughts through, after a period of time I go insane, forced to go against *my* nature.

O.W. said it's important to try to develop our opposites, strive to be a more rounded, mentally healthy person. He said I should continue to encourage Todd to express himself and search his brain for reason and answers, but to do so gently with patience.

I return home from the weekend with a much clearer insight into our home building struggle and into my dear husband's mind and heart (and my own). Certainly, more seems to be coming out of this project than we ever anticipated. The "why" is becoming clearer. We are getting to know each other as well as ourselves and that can only bring more love. I return to find Todd's letter on the kitchen table:

Dear Cindy,

    I believe I was avoiding the land for several reasons. Finishing the sauna was a great relief. It feels good not having it on a list of things to do. By starting the garden and cutting firewood, I felt I could knock out two more quick jobs, for all three need to get done. Going over to the land was like starting a whole new project, with no end in sight. I think I've refocused now. I look forward to working on the floor joists since our big sill logs are down . . . a little goal which will ultimately lead to the ridgepole sapling getting nailed in place one day.

    I also think I was a frustrated that things were not going as I would have liked them to. Fighting log weight and gravity was discouraging. There are better ways to move logs and I need to learn them. It will take some time experimenting to get things rolling smoothly. The work finale on the sauna was somewhat draining. I hope I can keep refreshed with other relief jobs—woodworking on rainy days, gardening, even some play days—going rafting, sailing, and camping out.

    I'm sorry for my blow-ups. I don't want to make excuses, for they are really uncalled for. I still feel that childish, uncontrollable German temper fly back into my brain on occasion.

    Hopefully, I'll have more self-control in the future. I suppose that particular German trait can be somewhat offset by some of my other traits, like being a hard worker. I feel blessed with my talents and the knowledge that I've acquired over the years. I was thinking today while turning over the soil by hand, what a wonderful grace it is to acquire wisdom. It's not learned by watching TV or by merely reading books, but by living. Time is the price you pay for wisdom, but then everyone goes through life at the same rate. Why not get wise by really living your life rather than merely passing through it? So, as I see it, we are not merely building a house, but learning, too. Maybe screwing up at times, but always learning, and we are becoming wiser. It's just when it gets so very difficult that it makes me wonder if it's all worth it.

Love, Todd

HINTS & TIPS:

- It is hugely beneficial to first build a small structure in the style and with the same kind of materials that you plan to use in your home—a garden shed or woodshed (in our case, a sauna). It will enable you to practice your new skills and make mistakes on a building that is not as crucial as your home.
- You do not need to know how to do every job nor possess every skill ahead of time when it comes to creating your home. Resources are readily available through books and videos, and you can learn skills as you go along. What you must have is a strong work ethic and the perseverance to see it through.
- Working closely with another person on a major project, such as building a log home, can be very stressful. It is important to have patience, be kind, try to communicate, work as a team. The skills you learn while navigating your relationship will mean just as much to your future happiness as a solid, beautiful home.

6
Rainy Spring

WE LIE IN BED A long time in the mornings. Legs wrap around legs like a loose braid. Hands hold hands resting on chests beneath the covers. It's our special time together. Todd knows that as soon as he stands upright, he won't slow down or rest until his day brings him back to this bed. Knowing this, it's often difficult for him to start.

But something is different today. Last night the clocks were turned ahead. Now there will be more daylight for work, and a friend is coming to help us build. We kick off the covers and pull on the work clothes that lie in a heap on the floor—worn day after day until a Laundromat visit is scheduled.

I make the bed and start breakfast. Into the lunch bucket goes the usual cheese, onion, bread, yogurt, and water bottle. Soon the truck is loaded for the day and we are ready to roll.

A brand-new job today—the floor joists. Before long, we move into a system. I take down knots on the logs with my chain saw, do some rough surface peeling here and there, and brush off the dirt with an old wool sock worn like a mitt. I draw lines on the log ends, square them off so they are all equal, and get ready to snap chalk lines. One entire side of the log will be flattened for the floorboards to rest on, while the other sides remain round. Two feet on each end will be squared and sawed so the joists can drop into the holes for them in the sill log and, hopefully, have them all be at the same height and be level. Todd wonders.

He turns his saw perpendicular to the log and slices off a layer like he's cutting a cake in half. Then he brushes the flattened surface with the teeth of his upright saw in long sweeping arcs. Thin shavings fly off, smoothing the log like he's creating art. Ron Brodigan taught him well.

While Todd flattens, our friend Mick Charowsky and I prep the logs. Mick is a big boy—6'2" with a solid 220-pound linebacker's frame. From his navy blue Penn State T-shirt, his forearms bulge massive and strong, a reminder of his tree surgeon days. The hair on the top of his head is going fast, so he rarely takes his Penn State baseball hat off. His face is handsome under the brim and his lips suck nicotine whenever he takes a break. Cigarettes are always in his pocket and his "shades" cover his eyes. Long cotton tube socks with red stripes extend up his leg while high leather work boots house his feet.

We met Mick a few years back at the Reading Area Community College where Todd and I taught an Adult Education Backpacking class. He was one of our first students and our passion for hiking must have infected him for he went on to also hike the entire Appalachian Trail and become a 2,000-miler. Mick loves to make music tapes, put together 1,000-piece puzzles, and watch football on television.

"Don't make me think!" he warns, when I ask him to help me figure. "I don't like to think." Yet he is very bright. I don't think he wants to feel responsible if he messes up on our house. Electronics fascinate him, and he can take them apart, repair whatever is broken, and put them back together again. His work is repairing Pepsi machines around the county. But electronics are a world away from log building. Mick is a bull, however. He comes because he's helpful and interested in the building process and because he likes to get a workout.

I roll up my white, baggy cotton pants from my pretzel factory days to cool off and my muscular calves swell out above my boots. My T-shirt is oversized for easy stretching to wipe my perspiring face and the cutoff sleeves are frayed and ragged. Loose hairs fall out of my braid and hang in my face. I pull my chainsaw cord and tear into the log. It doesn't give you a very feminine feeling, this log building stuff.

I'm just "one of the guys"—until mealtime, when I assume the role of cook on the building site. I pat burgundy-colored roadkill venison burger into patties and fry them on our two-dollar grill (yard sale special) which acts like a two-dollar grill, either licking the food with flames or smoking it.

It would probably help if we had charcoal instead of pine scraps for fuel. Since the spatula to flip the burgers was left at home, my choices are a wide, steel chisel or a piece of lath. The lath seems more hygienic.

Lunch is served on inverted Tupperware lids and pieces of used plastic wrap. Empty yogurt containers make fine cups. The "table" we sit at is a large rectangle of leftover concrete blocks piled four layers high, and our "seats" are also stacked block but only two layers high. "I can't get close enough to my sandwich!" I complain. "Well, pull your chair in!" Mick teases. Not the ultimate in fine dining, but good enough for a bunch of log builders!

As Todd finishes the joists, Mick and I lug them over and drop them into their chiseled-out slots—one end in the notched main beam, the other end in the sill log. Our system of communication is simple and to the point: "More?" "Ready?" "Okay!"

The levelness of the very first joist is tested by "Bossman" log builder Todd (as Mick calls him), as he slides his four-foot level up and down the flattened surface. The bubble remains perfectly in the middle of the lines no matter where on the log he moves it to. That same contented, satisfied look fills his face as when the concrete man called and said he did "a helluva job!"

Later that night, while Todd washes dishes and I dry, he explains the sudden appeal of log building. "Here's the problem," he says. "You have a log and need to get a flat surface on it to nail a floor on. How do you do it? How do you get a flat surface on something that isn't flat? By using concepts of leveling and squaring up! It's fascinating to me!" he beams.

"Next time things aren't going as well as you expected," I tell him, "or as fast as you expected, or you just can't figure things out and you have one of your little fits, I will remind you how this whole thing fascinates you."

When Todd crawls into bed tonight, tired and bone-weary but happy, he says, "I'd like to be able to work this hard until I'm one hundred and then drop dead."

Work continues on our floor joists, and, ever-so-slowly, flattened logs are dropped into their notches. The basement, no longer merely a big hole, looks like what it actually is—a framework for a floor. When viewed from certain angles, it almost appears to be a solid floor. Todd laughs and says, "We could just add a few more floor joists in between and we wouldn't have to bother nailing lumber down!"

I'm noticing that it takes me a little while to break into new jobs. I need good, precise instruction and I need tips to show me easier, more efficient ways of doing things. All these building skills are new to me. Today we're nailing oak planking to our floor joists as a subfloor while we build.

Todd wants to finish a solo job he had started, which means Mick and I will have to work together and lay boards. Since Mick prefers to work alone, I'm on my own. Todd takes exactly two minutes out of his time to show me the procedure. "You just lay the board down, measure, cut, and nail."

But I find it difficult to hold the board tightly in place against the last one. I need a Wonder Bar, a small, crowbar-like tool to hammer into the joist and yank back on, holding the board tightly against the last one. Mick is using the only one we have and isn't excited about sharing. He also has the only metal angle guide for drawing forty-five-degree lines. He is also using *my* chain saw and ear protectors. I do have my own hammer, but I cannot get my nail to go in straight. To add insult to injury, I cannot pull the crooked nail *out* of the plank. I go to Todd for help. Mick ignores me.

Watching closely while Todd nails, I realize he starts his nail on an angle, not straight up and down as I've been doing. And he doesn't come right down with the blow of his hammer but grazes it in the course of his swing. "No wonder my nails aren't going in straight. I'm not nailing correctly. Why didn't you show me?"

"I didn't think about it," he admits.

"Didn't your father ever show *you?*" I ask.

"No. I bent them for a long time, always marveling at how my father's went in so much straighter and easier. After a while, I finally figured it out for myself. I thought it was a secret."

"Thanks for passing on the knowledge," I say sarcastically.

I pick up his hammer, which is much heavier than my own, and find the added weight also makes it that much easier to nail.

It's been raining all morning, and I feel chilled and tired. My life has been packed too full lately with other commitments and I'm beginning to feel run down. I retreat to the truck to take a break, feeling helpless and not needed. I contemplate going home while my eyes fill with tears.

Todd approaches the truck cautiously, sensing there is something wrong. "I feel really tired, but I want to work. I want to work *with you*," I say.

"I'll be finished soon, and we can put boards down together."

There is an art to working with other people—not ordering like a boss and not forcing the other to merely be a gofer. Todd is cultivating this talent, for it wasn't too long ago on the batter boards where he admitted that he wasn't too good at it, either. I wipe my eyes and edge over to observe what Mick is doing and try to learn. Since he won't share *my* tools, I set him up, measure the next span for him, and find a board to fit that measurement. "There's too many people working here!" he barks rather gruffly.

It soon starts to rain, and Mick complains that he's no longer having any fun. He says he can't work with a rain jacket on and is thinking of going home. "I don't blame you," I support him. "I wouldn't be out here working in the cold and rain, either, if it weren't my house." He throws down his tools and heads out. I pull on my rain pants since it's falling harder and suddenly feel my fatigue fade! I am ready to work!

Todd gives me a simple job and I learn it and do it well. I bring the next board over, set it up, draw my angle line and prop it up for him to cut. He puts the first nail in, the hardest nail, and I follow, putting in the rest. The floor is going down! We flash each other smiles under our rain-drenched parka hoods. I feel close to my husband. I feel like his partner.

Mick is one of four brothers and no sisters and he's not accustomed to working with women, especially on a building project. The one dominant woman in his life, his mother, plays the traditional, subservient role and hasn't nailed down too many floors with the men. I understand his frustration of not knowing how to work with me nor wanting to learn how. I also honor my own feelings of wanting to be included in the construction process of *my* home and not wanting to be treated as if I were unnecessary.

I was fully aware that my husband and I would need to learn how to work together on the building site, but I wasn't thinking I would also need to learn how to work with *other* men. But Todd and I really appreciate and can use all the help that we can get, so here's to ramping up the learning! Mick's attitude caught me off guard. The next time I hope to respond more assertively.

As the weeks pass by, I get better at laying floor and cutting boards with my chainsaw. "You're just the cutest carpenter I've ever seen," Todd smiles, when I choke the saw's engine. If someone were around daily helping us build, I think I would really miss the closeness I feel with my husband. When just the two of us work, we are free to express our anger and frustration, as well as our playfulness and our love.

As soon as Todd awakes in the morning, he rolls over to look out the window. A question forms on the other one's lips, "Is it raining?" If the answer is "No," "How does the sky look?" quickly follows. Besides losing so much work time from the never-ceasing rain, mold is growing on our logs. Rainwater drips through the spaces in the floorboards, soaking the floor joists and main beam, which have already begun to rot.

Under the subfloor, the sun never shines, and it takes weeks of a dry spell for the logs to dry out. There is purple mold, yellow mold, white, brown, and black mold. Or is it fungi? Some forms into little wet balls, some into black powders. Some are spongy, slimy; others are dry. Todd is really worried.

I was *really* worried until he began to worry. Then I switched automatically to the role of optimist. We need to maintain a balance. "Look," I tell him. "The logs will only be exposed for two more years. We'll scrape the mold off."

The sawdust from cutting grooves and notches lies on the floor and collects water and could also really hasten rot, so Todd is a stickler for keeping the site clean. One man who built his own log home, *never* swept up the entire time. But because of how deep the sawdust got, he never needed scaffolding to reach his upper logs!

Our push broom has about half a dozen bristles left in it. When turned upside down, we can use the rubber edge as a sawdust scraper instead. I need to sweep in the same diagonal that the boards are running, for sweeping perpendicular only makes the dust hang up in the uneven boards.

"This is ridiculous!" I comment.

"When you begin spending fifty dollars a month on new brooms, you'll like that one, too," he replies. Everyone that sees it makes fun of it and makes comments about Todd's extreme frugality. Take today, for example. He's going to run out of gas. The can is almost empty. It only holds a gallon, and, because he must add a special premeasured solution to his gas, he must use up the old batch first to prevent water problems and blocked fuel lines. He'll run out of gas long before he'll run out of time and we'll have to quit early—just because he won't buy an additional gas can. His ways can be exasperating. I need to keep my sense of humor. When he's being ridiculous, he eventually sees it, but if he can get by with less, he does. On the other hand, because of Todd's frugality, we'll probably never go into debt, over this house or anything else.

The tax assessor has already been up, trying to get money out of us. He pulls up in a car unfamiliar to us and we look up from our work unemotionally.

"I was coming to see how far along you were. I can see you aren't ready to move in yet." We have two rounds of logs up and it looks more like the start of a corral than a home.

"Come back in three years," I tell him. He thinks I'm joking. "I'll see you next year," he says, and gets in his car and drives off.

"They don't waste any time," Todd mutters. We get a lot of gawkers driving up to our site, even though it's a half a mile off the main road, up a lane and out of sight. Who knows how they find out about what we're doing? One Sunday a man and his family drove up in a big, pink Lincoln Continental. He hopped out of the car all smiles and from the friendly way he behaved, I thought we must already know one another.

"Came up to check on your progress," he says, without introducing himself.

"How do you know about us?" I ask.

"Oh, word gets around. I live an hour away from here and stop in whenever I'm in the area." Well, that's just great. When our oak planks were delivered, two walked off after we left for the day. It's beginning to give us the creeps. I can feel myself shifting from my normal, very friendly self to a more private person like my husband. Because of our home's uniqueness, I fear it may be a real struggle to hang on to what little privacy we have.

We were visited by some hunters last fall. We knew they were in the forest nearby because we heard their pellets pinging the leaves right above our heads after they shot. We yelled to them, unsure why Todd's revving chainsaw didn't give it away that there were humans up here. They came up to the building site and asked, "What fer book did you git this out of?" I was tempted to say "*Popular Mechanics*" but didn't bother. We told them that although we did not post "No Hunting" signs, hunting right over the hill where we are building is too close for comfort and safety.

We persevere through the rainy spring and progress ever so slowly. We close our eyes to the mold and the rot and keep laying logs on top of logs. The sooner the building gains height, the sooner the protective roof can go on. Folks ask how high the building is. "That depends on where you stand," Todd says. "From the basement floor, it's very tall. We could put a roof on and live in it right now. From the ground outside, it's over your head. But standing in the house, on the floor, it's only up to your shins!"

HINTS & TIPS:

- Our floor joists were made of small logs (log tops) which were hand-flattened and took a tremendous amount of time. Dimensional lumber would have made laying a floor so much easier and faster (but more expensive). This is one place that you can save considerable time if money is not as important as getting your home built.
- When it comes to doing anything that is extremely strenuous, and involves a tremendous amount of mental work besides, like building a log home, listen to your body. If it signals that it's

overwhelmed and needs a break, honor it. That is when accidents happen—from serious fatigue. Running yourself down without the proper rest will make you susceptible to illness, which will hamper your progress even more. Work to maintain moderation in all aspects of your work.

- If you can pace yourself and take breaks away from the work site, you will enjoy your home building project much more, especially since the duration of the task could be monumental. It is not a frivolous act to go on a vacation or take mini trips if that is what will renew your spirit and make continued building more fun.
- You may find it challenging to work with others when folks come to help. Keep in mind that it is *your* home that you are building, and you are in charge. There only needs to be one boss, and it is the homeowner. Bear in mind, however, that most folks coming to help want to be a help so it's up to you to make them feel valued, find work for them to do so they can stay busy and feel needed. Learn to delegate jobs, be assertive and straightforward in explaining the best way you know how to do a job, so their learning curve is shorter, and they feel successful.

7
Dog Days

LOG PEELING IS A WINTERTIME, cold-weather job. It pushes your cardiovascular system and raises your body temperature in a matter of minutes. It's eighty-five degrees this May day and I don't care to raise my body temperature by one degree. But it's time to peel logs. The walls must go up!

Our logs are very dry. They have checks (cracks) half an inch deep in them. These thin-barked spruce trees lost their protective bark long ago as they were transported one time too many. Because of their missing bark, the wood dried out considerably. We are actually shaving off a layer of wood with our heavy drawknife blades, not sliding them under bark and scraping it off. The surface has become black with dirt and mildew so the top layer of wood must be shaved off. I stop peeling and look at my swollen hands. Blood surges through the pronounced veins, muscles bulge. My rings are tight and oval shaped, flattened from applying pressure and using my hands to lift and carry heavy objects. There are calluses on my palms. They are tender and sore to the touch, for I use them to pound mallets into chisels and hack away at hard sappy knots. What will my hands look like when this house is completed?

Todd's hands have grown tremendously since he began to build. Like those of the old Pennsylvania German welder, Amos Stoltzfus, who did some work on our tools, his hands were like grizzly bear paws with fingers so wide and muscular they were perpetually spread out. There are muscles in your hands, of course, like every other part of your body. Our feet grew larger as our muscles developed from thousands of miles of long-distance backpacking. In only two years of marriage, Todd has already had his wedding band enlarged.

Todd and I fetch leather gloves for protection. "It hurts, doesn't it?" I say. The knots are what kill my hands. They are so much harder and denser than the other wood on the tree, and they jar my drawknife with their resistance. Working on a tough knot, especially at the end of the day when you are tired and hungry is like cruising on a downhill backpacking and suddenly having the trail sprint you uphill for a short stretch. No matter how slight the incline, hunger and weakness surge through your body. That little demand of energy drains you.

Todd peels like a madman. From a standing position, he bends over the log as he straddles it and moves that drawknife furiously back and forth at top speed. When a log is short and not very heavy, his shaving motion moves it right off the skids. I sit on the other end for him and peel, so the log remains more stationary, but his frenzied speed drives me nuts. I peel slowly and steadily. I pace myself and sit on the log, but it makes me feel like I've ridden on a hard-seated bicycle all day. My back needs a rolling on a log every now and then to crack my bones and bend my spine back the other way. When Todd finally stops, he's breathing heavily, as if he just ran a sprint. "You sound like you're hyperventilating," I tell him. Even peeling at a slower pace like my own is incredibly taxing on my cardiovascular system. Sometimes it feels as though huge hands were around my chest, squeezing it very hard. When we peel, our chest muscles and pectorals are really doing a job, too, besides our hearts.

Three seconds of lifting work also makes my heart pound out of my chest. My stomach feels nauseated and I feel like I've worked out for an hour. There's a limit to my strength, at least until I build it up more. So often it's just the two of us up here, though, and I have to do what I can. This makes it even more evident that having babies must simply wait until the last log is lifted.

I stop peeling for a moment and try to cool off in the afternoon heat. Sweat runs in my eyes and burns. My glasses slide down and hang on the tip of my nose. Black dirt lines encircle my neck. I pour water over my head to cool off. Todd looks at me and laughs out loud. "You look rough."

"You don't look much better," I inform him. He is wearing a ripped T-shirt that is so thin all the cotton fibers have been worn away and just the gauzy, transparent polyester remains. One arm is sleeveless, the other half gone. There's another hole in his back large enough for his head to fit through. He wears it because it's the coolest shirt he owns. I don't know why he bothers. I'm tempted to throw it out, but my mother used to do that to some of my old hiking clothes that had sentimental value and I resented her for it.

His muscular pectorals stick out and flex as he lifts his helmet onto his head and reaches to pull his ear protectors down. His dark hair is wild and long. Curls hang down the nape of his neck, form ringlets on his perspired brow, and stick out from his orange helmet. It's almost long enough to gather into a ponytail, but there is never any time to cut it.

Since the rainy season has ended, we are up here every possible minute of the day. Not much else goes on—except building. A Crock Pot meal every now and then. A floor swept. The only place it gets washed is where the cat's water spills occasionally—the cleanest part of the floor. As Todd cooks on our grimy two-burner Coleman stove, he says, "Getting pretty bad." He doesn't say, "Maybe, you ought to think about cleaning it." He knows better. He leaves for work and the next minute I am doing my work—painting and writing. Every other minute of the day, I am up working on logs with him. I can't do it all, and he knows it. I tell him that "a clean house is a sign of a wasted life." (I saw that on a T-shirt one time.) And as far as the gross-looking stove goes, my reply is, "Perhaps it's time to start putting the lid down then," and we laugh.

As we take a break from peeling, Todd and I watch as the shade line creeps closer and the sun, which feels like our enemy this time of year, moves further across the sky. We're peeling our logs on the edge of our forested land—"the shaving factory" we call the spot. The log transporter couldn't get his truck back to our actual building site since we cut as few trees as possible. We want to live in the woods. Why cut a huge hole in them to set a house?

We're trying to time our workweek so that we get a half of a round of logs peeled by Friday. Sometimes, we are blessed with some workers on the weekends and try to plan our heaviest work for them. What takes Todd and me hours to complete can be done in minutes with two other strong men.

The helpers come for different reasons. Mick comes to get strong and tanned. He likes to peel logs in the sun and doesn't feel he gets enough of a workout during the week. Rick Muntone, another one of our backpacking class students, comes for the diversion and to learn something that he's never done before. Steve Spadafore, another long-distance hiker and an engineer, comes because he entertains the idea of building a log house of his own someday. Working on our home, observing the struggles we go through and how we solve them,

helps Steve determine whether this incredible endeavor is really for him or not. Peeling logs isn't our helpers' favorite job, but no matter how much Todd and I plan, it often falls into the work agenda for the weekend. Sunday is always the hardest day for our weekend help. They give their all on Saturday and are wiped out one day later.

"He'll be busy from now on," I say to Todd, teasing Steve. "That's okay," I joke, "We're used to one-night stands."

"I'm not discouraged yet," Steve replies. "My eyes are open to the reality of it now. It's a whole lot slower than I ever imagined, and a whole lot more hard work. I know I can build a frame house *at least* now, once I've seen how difficult a log house is."

Todd asks our helpers, "Would you do this job for minimum wage?"

Rick replies, "For twelve bucks an hour and health benefits, *maybe*."

"Dental and eye care, too," Steve adds. "Then maybe we'd be ready to talk!"

Peeling is damn hard work. There's no way around it. Todd and I have the advantage of doing it often instead of a weekend here and a weekend there like these guys. We get stronger and more skilled. I always find myself going over their logs, for they leave choppy gash marks with their drawknives—not having the rhythm and depth control of the blade down pat. I used to feel worried that they'd be insulted by my going over their work, but I tell them I do it to everyone, including Todd. I must look at these walls a whole lot longer than any of our helpers. They understand, and it's good for their pride.

These few single, male friends are about our only positive reinforcement on this project. Most folks tell us we are crazy to work so hard. They say that we never seem to get anywhere and that four years dedicated to a project is an extraordinary chunk of your life—as though we are wasting it. My eighty-year-old Polish-German grandmother came up with my sister, Joann, for a surprise visit the other day. When the car approached the "shaving factory," my chainsaw was running, and I was taking down knots on the logs. When I turned off my saw, my grandmother was crying and coming for a hug, saying that we work "too

damn hard," that she feels sorry for us, and that she wishes one of us would get sick so we could take a break and have a rest! She, who just repaired her own roof at eighty years old and who lived through the Great Depression and mothered her twelve brothers and sisters while her mom worked, thinks that we have it hard!

While my grandmother admires our perseverance and work ethic, she wants us to have an easy and comfortable life. But she wouldn't be the dynamo she is today if *she* had had such an easy and comfortable life. She's knows that we're doing this hard work by choice but the "why" of it is not clear to her. She's not alone with that thought. There's not much of a beautiful house to encourage and psych even Todd and I up sometimes, convincing us that it's all worthwhile. But we persevere, buoyed by each other's dedication, and as the spring melts into the hot days of summer, it is time to find more logs, as our full load of Dory's logs has been used up.

HINTS & TIPS:

- When looking for drawknives to purchase, the heavier, sturdier drawknives will work best. (Flea markets and antique tool shops are good places to look for used tools.) Small, narrow knives will only frustrate you when it comes to working on those large, tough knots. Make sure your knives are sharp, especially if your logs were dragged through dirt and the bark is caked with soil. They will dull quickly.
- Rubbing alcohol works great to get sap off your skin, which we usually did at the end of the day. Consider wearing longer shorts in the summer as sap on hair can be painful.
- Chainsaws, like any tool, should be properly maintained. A dull chainsaw will put tremendous wear and tear on the bar and your body. A sharp saw cuts fast and saves time.

8

The Big Wait

The Pennsylvania Forest Service distributes a directory of sawmills and loggers. I thumb through the pages and star the likely candidates in nearby counties. I insist that Todd make the calls as he knows best what we need, but his childhood phone fear rears its ugly head again.

"Do you cut logs for log homes?" he asks. "Okay, thank you," and hangs up.

"Of course, they don't normally cut trees for log homes. You know the few stands of softwoods around here get trucked to the Glatfelter Paper pulp mill, in southern York county (where Todd's ancestors and relatives hail from). "Probably no one in Pennsylvania ever built a home like ours. The loggers need to be talked with awhile, tell them what we're doing, get them interested."

"It's perfectly obvious that they don't want to help us," Todd rationalizes. Well, no kidding. It's much easier for them to simply not deal with us. But it doesn't help our situation. We still need trees, or we can't build. Then he adds, "Look, do you want to call? I hate to talk on the phone." I am reminded of Dr. Lacy's saying, "Gifts differing," and I take over the phone calling. Some of the skills we are learning will take years to master.

Before long, I find Randy Bloc in the Hegins Valley of Schuylkill County. He sounds pretty young on the phone, although he speaks with a very strong Pennsylvania German accent. He doesn't think he can help us, although he is intrigued with our project. I convince him that he can help us, but he is concerned with fitting us into his schedule. He is currently involved with a contract for the paper mill and can't get the logs we want right away. I tell him "soon," not "immediately."

Randy is going to look at the stand of trees he's cutting now and see how many tall, broad ones he can find us. On our end, we'll figure out the exact lengths we need, and we'll get back to each other. On our second phone conversation, he chats for twenty minutes, giving explicit instructions to drive to the woods that he's cutting. We both feel it is best to walk the tract and have a look at the trees, making sure that they are not too skinny, have little taper so we can get two wall lengths out of one tree, and do not have big bells like Dory's logs. Randy reminds us more than once to stop at the summit on our drive across the mountain, to take in the beautiful view. We're impressed with his sensitivity toward nature and his wanting to share it.

Randy Bloc is short, but his big barrel chest, muscular arms, and slim tight stomach make him look like a power lifter. He wears a faded, orange Husqvarna chainsaw helmet with longish, frizzy hair sticking out the back, wire glasses, and has a nice-sized space between his two front teeth.

We all shake hands, and Todd and I proceed to follow him up the forested land. He plows through the woods like a bull moose. His muscular legs take long steps, twice our stride. He seems to float uphill, never looking back to see if we can keep up, somehow assured that everyone can move over brush and downed trees like him. "We're tree shopping," we say to each other, breathless. Down below, we see only twisted, spindly scotch pines. Up higher, Randy shows us beautiful white pines—straight, uniform, wide. We stop and look them up and down. "We can get two lengths out of each tree and there's very little taper." We tell Randy our horror story with Dory's logs—the gashes from his grabbers, the deep saw cut marks, the skinny logs with the big-belled bottoms. "I know what you're looking for," he says, and Todd and I feel confident that he'll do a good job.

One month later, we're on our fourth round of Dory's old spruce logs. New pine logs should come in a week, according to Randy, so we're hustling to finish up with these spindly, dried-out logs. All log homes are made from softwoods, as their R-value is higher, from the air trapped in their larger (than hardwood) cells, and, they are more rot resistant as well as lighter to handle. White pines are even better than spruce, which is what Randy will be cutting for us.

Work is not going so well today. Todd has been super sensitive lately. This morning while we peeled, I came to two terribly difficult, large knots and said, "While you're at it, get these two," as he was feeling strong and peeling at his usual maniac speed while I wilted. He looks at me and says, "I'm busting my ass and you think it's not good enough."

"What?" I reply. "You're crazy. I think you work too hard and you know it. Something else is wrong."

I begin to set up a log and measure the gap while he brings the tools over.

"What's wrong with you lately?" I ask.

"I'm just tired of working both jobs," he says. "It's really getting to me."

All Todd does is work. We wake up and he builds for half a day. Then he goes into his paying work and pushes lumber through a table saw, making kitchen cabinets, for the rest of the day. It's even more difficult for him when he doesn't have a lot of orders to fill, for the time really crawls. If he can, he works at a frenzied pace, cutting four to six hundred doors to everyone else's two hundred, for it keeps him occupied and passes the time. "Brainless work for the brainless," he says. A means to an end for him, that's all. His saving grace is the hefty paycheck that goes toward building supplies.

"Eight more months," I tell him.

"Why eight more months?" he asks, and I march over to my purse in the truck and pull out a savings account book. "I know what's in there," he says.

Earlier in the month, I showed him an account that I've been stashing money into over the past year. Before any bills are paid, I take fifty dollars out of every one of his checks and put it in this account for his woodworking shop tools. He'll have a few thousand dollars by next year to buy a fully equipped shop. He knew about that. What he doesn't know is that I've been saving *other* money that *I* made in another secret account so he can quit and we can live off it and work on the house. Tears fill his eyes. "Oh honey, thank you for being so understanding and patient with me."

"Thank *you* for working so hard for me. We're going on a hike next summer, too." I tell him. "We're going to need it. Eight hundred miles in the Sierra Nevada Mountains of California."

We know the logs have rot. We know the roof needs to go on as soon as possible and we should keep working straight through until it's complete. But we also more strongly believe in taking care of our mental health. We will need and deserve a break by next summer.

"I can hang in there, honey," he says as we hug. So, our goal is one round of logs per month. That's thirteen logs in each round. Hopefully, we'll get the building under roof before we leave for California next summer.

When I wake up this morning, I'm not feeling great but go over to build anyway. "My stomach feels bad," I announce, when I lean against a log to scribe. "Lie down," Todd says. I try to get comfortable in a corner of the house on the uneven oak planks, while little chips of wood bite into my skin and plant themselves in my hair. When Todd walks across the floor with his high-heeled, heavy logging boots, it jars my brains and makes me feel ten times worse. From my spot in the future living room, I watch Todd work. I watch how he uses his body when he saws a notch. The heavy Echo chainsaw rests against his leg. He moves his entire body in a swinging motion along with the back-and-forth swing of the saw bar in the notch he's cutting. When he gets the saw tip in the highest part of the curve, where he must hold it to do some concentrated chipping, his abdomen muscles contract and his stomach curves inward, working to hold the saw in place. Such grace and control.

When the notch is complete and the motor is cut, the sounds of summer return. Cicadas buzz in the treetops. Gnats fly around my head. I look around the shallow "walls" of our house and try to imagine life within them. In my spot where I lie will be an easy chair by the bookshelf. From here, I can see myself in the open kitchen, stoking the wood cook stove. A child leans over the balcony rail on the second floor and yells down to her mother. Daily life in our new home. It seems like it will never happen. Four rounds high is a long way from a finished house with a roof.

We are building a home: a warm, tight, dry structure to house our children and build a future. These walls will hear babies cry, and ring with their laughter and happy chatter. The children aren't here yet, but we know they will probably be coming, along with hard times and good times, all occurring within the boundary of these log walls that my husband and I put in place with our calloused hands. So much living to look forward to. It helps us get through the feelings of frustration and doubt.

The sun is creeping toward me as I lay in my thin strip of shade against the wall. Our building is shaded in the early morning and in the late afternoon hours. At high noon, when the sun passes over the hole in the forest canopy that we cut out for our house, we get struck by the scorching rays. Todd is worked up over his saw. He's pulling the cord twelve times to start it but the engine won't turn over. Vapor lock. The gas boils in the tank when it's this hot out. How he hates it when it won't perform. He dresses himself up in his safety outfit—Kevlar chaps to protect his legs, leather gloves, helmet with ear protectors and face shield. Then he has to take it all off when the saw won't start and let it sit. He moves to another job while the saw cools in the shade.

"What are you thinking, honey?" I ask from the floor.

"Nothing, just watching the wood come out as I clean out the groove. Actually, I was thinking how long it would take me to build this house all by myself, if my wife were sick every day. So, I better not get her pregnant because she could have morning sickness every day, all day!"

Before too many days pass by, I am back in commission, but Todd catches the same illness, some kind of viral flu. Altogether, the illness sets our log work back by a full week.

But the new logs never came anyway. We're at these loggers' mercy. They don't need us. The paper mill wants their trees. We are just more work and hassle for them.

Since we must wait for more logs, Todd decides it's a good time to make a new contraption for moving the heavy, green logs that should arrive someday soon. The two of us just can't muscle them up anymore. The derrick he's making is designed in the shape of a wooden tripod, fifteen feet high, resting on a triangular base. There is a manual boat winch secured on top of the apex and a hand crankshaft at waist height. The monster rolls around on casters, is pushed against a log wall and will supposedly hoist up a log to place on the building. When Todd is about finished with the construction, I ask, "Is that narrow enough to fit in the rooms between our interior log walls?" His face loses its expression and he proceeds to take the thing apart to cut it down and reduce its width. After it's complete, we steer it across the floor, getting hung up on uneven floor planks and, as a test, attach our set of wheels for moving logs to the cable. I crank it up onto the building and he cheers. Then I lower it again and he hops on top of the wheels for added weight. The whole derrick tips forward, lowering Todd and the wheels to the ground. "Oh great! It will never lift a twenty-five-foot, eight-hundred-pound green log. I can't deal with it," Todd exclaims, "This makes me sick." And with that episode, he proceeds to get a relapse of this strange flu.

Over a month has gone by and still no logs. Todd and I cut quite a few truckloads of firewood while we wait and move nearly four thousand pieces of used slate for our roof. But still, every day that passes, we grow more frustrated. Every time we make a trip to our land, we see our house just sitting there, never gaining any height nor making any

progress. Two more weeks go by. I call Randy every couple of days, trying not to appear frustrated. There are lots of reasons we have no logs: he went off that cut and onto another job; workers got hurt; brakes failed; trucks rolled; a truck "broke in half."

After two entire months of no progress, Randy finally calls to tell me the truck is loaded and he's coming tomorrow. Todd and I sit in our pickup by the highway, waiting to escort him up our driveway, but his estimated arrival time comes and goes. Every time a truck strains up the hill, we turn and look. Then all of a sudden, we see this red truck with a boom and a huge pile of logs on the back, creeping along very slowly. We can hardly believe our eyes! He's here!

The electric wires sag low and scrape his log tops, looking like they'll snag on a branch any second. When he pulls into our driveway, I walk up to his truck and say, "We almost gave up on you."

"I had a terrible time getting here. I woke up with a horrible migraine headache and had to pull off the road twice because I couldn't stand the pain. Then a truck going the opposite way flashed its lights to me so I pulled over and walked a mile, looking for a cop, for I was so overloaded and would surely get fined."

At the edge of the field, Randy controls the boom's grabbers with grace and gentleness, placing each log straight in line on a perfect pile. Sitting up high on his truck, he makes that boom perform magic.

Randy's log price is great. Like Dory, he is charging us pulp prices or what he could get for the trees if he drove them to the paper mill down in southern Pennsylvania. Like Dory, Randy is helping us out because he wants to see us get a beautiful log home. But unlike Dory's logs, which cost $900 to haul them two times by another company, Randy isn't charging us anything for his hauling time, just twenty-eight dollars a ton. That's how we buy materials for our home construction . . . by the ton! I tell him not to sell himself short, to make sure he's covered. We need him to continue doing business with us. When he tells us he could have been fined $1,500 if he would have gotten caught, I ask, "Would it have been worth it?"

"I wanted to get you off my back!" he replies and laughs.

"We could have done with ten less logs! Don't stick your neck out like that again."

Over and over he says how sorry he is that it took so long. "If I would have cut your logs any sooner, it really would have screwed me up and I would have lost a lot of money." That's understandable. I was just looking for honesty along the way. We would have built an outbuilding, or laid the block for our sunroom, but we never wanted to start a big project because the logs were always 'coming in a few days.'"

"I had a half a notion to tell you to forget it," he admits, but he didn't, and that means a lot to us.

After another hour of chatting, him telling stories about how he got started in his logging business and giving us detailed instructions on how to get to his home if we are ever in the neighborhood, he goes out to his truck and climbs in. He looks out of the cab window and says to us: "There you go, one house . . . I guess."

He's close. It's part of a house. We'll still need a good two more loads and who knows what kind of circus it will be getting them.

HINTS & TIPS:

- Before you even decide whether or not to build a log cabin or home, first explore the possibilities of where you can attain logs. If you live in a forested state, there should be loggers with whom you can connect. Many loggers work with the state and national forestry departments as independent contractors and are hired to thin their stands. If you have a very hard time locating trees, and they have to be trucked in from far, the cost of your logs may rise exponentially.
- Work out your log-lifting mechanisms way ahead of time. Do your research, purchase your materials or your machine so you do not have to take time out from building when you hit a wall and can no longer raise your logs.
- Use a chainsaw that is comfortable for you to handle. A larger saw will cut faster, but extreme control is needed when cutting notches and grooves. Generally, a sixteen-inch bar is ideal for log work. The longer the bar, the less control you have for fine work.
- Incorporating a stub wall into your house design when you have a long span will enable you to use shorter logs of more uniform diameter. By splicing them and hiding the cut inside the stub wall, you can use two shorter logs and they will be easier to manage. Doorways and windows also allow for shorter logs. If you offset your wall as we did in our design (by incorporating a jog on the north and south sides of our home), this will also enable the use of shorter, more uniform logs, but it will increase the number of notches you must saw.

THE FOURTH YEAR
1988

9

The New Logs

WHAT WE HAD HOPED FOR and dreamed about for so many months has finally come true—we have new logs—fresh and green and easy to peel; long and wide and beautiful to look at. But they have quickly become the source of all our frustration, fighting, and fear.

Our first job is to push around the new log pile and select logs for the next half round. We work on half of a round of logs at a time, i.e., either the logs on the north and south walls, or the logs on the east and west walls. We grow our log home half a round at a time. Before we go back to the log pile to select our logs and bring them back, we have to take measurements on the last notches on the building, which this next half round of logs will be covering. The entire building, all the log walls, must remain even and grow taller at the same rate. Therefore, careful measuring is a must. Butt ends are bigger than top ends and they need to alternate on each wall. If there is a six-inch section of log remaining above its notch, you can't put a seven-inch log over top of it or you will only have one inch of wood remaining. We measure each notch and decide what width log will work best over top. Todd and I work in a team, measuring and figuring and writing down log lengths and widths that we'll be looking for once we go out to the log pile.

Unfortunately, the specific logs we need lie are on the very bottom of the four-layer-deep pile and it takes some digging to bring them to the surface. We wedge our pointed peavey poles under a log and try to push it up, out of the space it fell into, between two logs, and then roll it off the pile. This hard upper-body work requires either Todd and I to push or hold a log in place while the other gets a bite with the peavey hook. We must think fast and move fast, jump out of the way if a log begins to roll, quickly move a foot as a log does the unexpected, or pull a hand back just as our fingers are about to be crushed. So much of our success depends on mutual assistance, working in sync with each other, knowing what the other person will do next or anticipating how the log will act, without taking the time to discuss and map out procedures. It's very difficult for me. I still need Todd to communicate what he will do next, to say, "I'm going to push this end of the log so it swings around to the right." Then I will know to get my body out of the way and where to brace the other end of the log. My mind isn't accustomed to figuring out methods of levers, weights, and counterbalancing, I need Todd to say, "One, two, three, PUSH!" so I can contribute my strength at the best time.

It isn't always easy or convenient for him to stop and report every move he is going to make and predict every move the log will make. "I want them to move fast," he says in frustration. "I want to put them down on the building fast and see it go up fast." As of late, he is obsessed with getting work accomplished. Obsessed with getting jobs behind us instead of so very much ahead. These heavy logs don't go *anywhere* fast, however.

He says, "I think it's quite evident what I am going to do with the next log and how it will behave without needing to report to you." Not so. It's going to take a lot of repetition for me to predict his behavior or anticipate all the possibilities of a moving log.

Besides getting smarter, I desperately need to get stronger. As Todd goes to the outhouse, I sit down with my book, *Having A Baby Over Thirty,* to read a few quick paragraphs, but mostly to rest. This does not please him at all. I learn this when we come up to the building pulling a log and he stops at a rope on the ground, one and a half yards from the spot that we should have stopped at.

"What's the matter?" I ask.

"The rope. You could have moved the rope."

"Me?"

"Yes. You could think ahead as to what things need to be done, instead of reading your book." I look at him with anger and hurt in my eyes. "Every now and then I need to rest. At the end of each day, every part of my body aches, even my face and eyeballs from the stress. You resent the fact that I sit down and take breaks, don't you?"

"No," he says, but his grin gives him away.

"Believe it or not," I admit, "I get tired. You think I'm a slouch."

"That's not true," he says. "I thought you were sitting there because you were bored. I have a hard time believing people get tired when I never do."

"Well, you're some sort of superman. You're fanatical about work and don't know when to stop. Don't expect the same from others. I'm doing the best job I can," and the tears begin to flow.

"I'm sorry, honey. I've never been so overwhelmed as this. It's really tough. It's more than I can handle."

"Try to remember that I'm not your enemy."

"You need a stronger husband," he says.

"You need a *man* for a wife!"

"Hurry up and get stronger, honey."

Not only do I lack the required stamina, but my mental strength is at an all-time low. At the land, I catch myself walking around with a frown and a tensed brow. I try to close my eyes and tell myself to relax and unwind and meditate for a few minutes. It all seems so strenuous and difficult now. After our initial struggle of learning how to move our first batch of logs and put up our first round of logs, log work became increasingly easier. The logs were so dry and so light and progress seemed to flow. That's all over now with these new, green logs. I feel fatigued as soon as I drive to the building site. When we go out to the pile to muscle our green logs around, I am flooded with anxiety.

I noticed something really strange today. We had an extremely heavy log to move and when I looked at it, I was overwhelmed with a feeling of suffocation. I could not cope with working through the logistics of moving the log with Todd. It all seems like such a tremendous struggle. Lately, when I look in the mirror, I look so old, so very fatigued. I'm not taking care of myself. Todd and I fight nearly every day at the building site. Never any other time, just up there. I hate it. At first, it was amusing and entertaining to observe Todd as he learned to express himself and open up. It was fascinating to me, and I encouraged him to speak his mind. Now it's grown old. It seems so personal now, as if he is attacking *me*, resenting *me*, and it hurts. It actually makes me feel ill when we do not speak kindly and lovingly to each other.

Todd looks so forlorn when we fight. His brow wrinkles and his eyes stare dead and cold. Then his body gets stiff like a board and he becomes immobilized. I can almost see his hair graying before my eyes. Fighting feels like poison, like it's eating me. I cannot live like this. Perhaps, that is why I do not even want to go up to building site. I see the logs coming in between my husband and me and it makes me not care for them. Working on the house could mean another fight. As long as we stay away, I rationalize, we will be close. We better figure out how to deal with this because we have tougher times ahead.

It's interesting to observe how Todd and I take turns becoming overwhelmed with the building, losing interest in the work, and falling apart emotionally. The stronger one has to step up and find the strength (either physical or emotional) to usher both through the hard time, knowing that eventually the tables will turn again, and we will reverse roles. I imagine that is how it will be throughout our marriage, and our lives together, as challenges arise and struggles demand more from us. This building site is our training ground, our school, for life ahead.

Up to this point, we placed our logs onto the building by hand. We often could plan this step for weekends when friends sometimes came to help. But they have not been around for many weeks. Mick had a soda machine fall on his back. Rick is into the hunting season. One guy just got a girlfriend and another watches football on TV. It's now just Todd, myself, and "Derrick"—our wooden tripod with the manual boat winch that Todd built to hoist logs onto the building. We must still solve the problem of the whole contraption tilting forward from the weight of a *light* log. I used to stand on its back end for added weight, but these new, heavy logs would project me into the air and sail me over the building.

Todd cuts wider spaces between our oak floor planks and we wrap a bicycle lock cable around the derrick, through the slits in the floor. I lock it to a floor joist. As I crank a heavy log up, the cable stretches and crackles under the weight. The handle is very difficult to turn and hold on to, for the tension is extreme. Both of us are afraid of me letting go. I'm afraid of breaking my teeth and jaw from the flying handle, Todd of being crushed under a falling log. He is positioned on the ground, beside the house, under the log, holding the ends of two ropes that are tied around each end of the log so he can attempt to pull it away from the building. Often it slams into the foundation anyway. We're beginning to realize that this is not the safest and easiest way to get the logs up anymore, but right now it's all we have to work with. Todd is putting off building the cable skyline that will hoist logs into the air and move them across the building until he absolutely *has* to. The time lost from log building to design and rig a skyline, plus the mental energy involved to figure out how to do it, makes him settle with what we have: the derrick.

Our log building teacher, Ron Brodigan, went over the different ways of moving logs while at school, but every building site is different, and every work "crew" is different—we had a team at school, here it is mostly just Todd and I left to figure how to move these heavy monsters ourselves.

Getting the logs onto the building is only one of our major problems to solve. Once they've been scribed, getting them down to the floor to cut the grooves is another. "How did we do it before? How did we move the log under it?" The procedure we used before won't work now. This log is green. This is a new situation. Todd's brow furrows and his eyes grow wide with concentration. He doesn't look at me. He looks at the problem, and doesn't take his eyes off it, waiting for it to speak to him and give him the answer. It usually does.

I look the situation over and an idea might flash through my mind, without thinking it entirely through. I don't actually set it up in my mind, and try to predict how the log will act, as Todd does. I don't have enough experience with weights, balance, levers, pulleys and ramps to do all that. I merely offer suggestions. I am convinced that that is the entire secret of this log building racket—figuring how to move the logs and put them where we want them. Once we figure something out, we can use that "tool" in our toolbox of how to move logs, but nearly every log seems different. For one, the height of the building changes constantly, and that impacts each new round of logs.

The skill of the actual scribing and sawing is only a matter of practice and time. We get faster and more precise. We get stronger and better able to hold the tools and work them. Todd and I are super at our individual jobs. Our logs fit so very tight. They roll over with an amazing thud. We bend over and look for gaps, for thin lines of daylight showing where the log might be held up by a knot or a wood chip, but we never find any. Ron Brodigan taught us well. "One moose hair" of a gap is all that was allowed at log building school, and we try to hold that same high standard. Our logs fit perfectly, the top log curving beautifully around the bulges of the one below. But this business of moving them to where we want them is a constant, ever changing challenge.

Todd says ideally, he would like it if I were an equal log builder, equal in problem solving as well as skill and strength. It would give him some relief from always being responsible and in charge. But he forgets that he is really a solo worker and thinker and prefers it this way. Nor would he be accumulating the self-esteem and personal confidence that he is if he weren't in charge. Personally, levers, pulleys, ramps, and chainsawing simply don't interest me *as much* as they do him.

"You *seem* to get excited over figuring out how to move logs," he comments.

"I am, but you are *tremendously* interested." We have shared so much together in our lives: gardening, backpacking, cooking and baking, and now building this house. Of course, I want to share this, too, but I'm also aware that my passion does not quite match his. That's hard for both of us because our interest and desire to work are not always at the same level.

As the days pass and the next round of logs slowly go up, the tension seems to subside a bit. I initiate "no-fighting kisses" throughout the day. I forget my own frustration and concentrate on keeping Todd calm and support him when he's perplexed over a procedure. If he is calm, I am calm. When he begins to get anxious, I use different tricks to get him to smile. Sometimes I pull my camera out and say I need some personality profiles of grouchy faces to round out my log building slideshow. I come in real tight to focus on his face, and instruct, "Don't smile! No smiling allowed!" and he usually breaks out in a grin. Sometimes I do a cheer adapted from a local high school, in the Pennsylvania German town of Kutztown. In my best German accent, I sing, "Ring Bologna once, Ring bologna twice, Ra! Ra! Log Building, Geez that's nice!"

If all else fails, I pull down his zipper and pull out his manhood and say, "It needs some air." His face immediately breaks out in a grin and says, "Oh honey, it's not time for that." No kidding. There's no time for grouchiness, either.

I do "dance around him," as my grandmother says, but I refuse to allow him to stay mired in a miserable mood for very long. Too much wasted life. My grandmother said that my grandpop would completely ignore her for weeks while in a bad mood. That would never fly in my family. Todd often cannot articulate in words what is causing the distress. I sometimes have to ask, "Can you please tell me why we are *both* unhappy because your mood directly affects mine and I don't have a clue why *I* am unhappy?" He might be dealing with a bad headache and thinks he ought to "muscle through" and ignore it. It might be a fear, either real or imagined, but nevertheless, stuck in his mind, mulling over, with no one else to help him through it.

Sometimes the best way to deal with the work challenge is to walk away from it and take a break. A vacation with my family at the ocean seems to be in order about now. Our lives can slow and there is time for long walks on the beach, lots of hand-holding, hugging, and talking. We talk about children mostly. As we are surrounded by our nieces and nephews here on vacation, they make us think about what lies ahead after the house is complete.

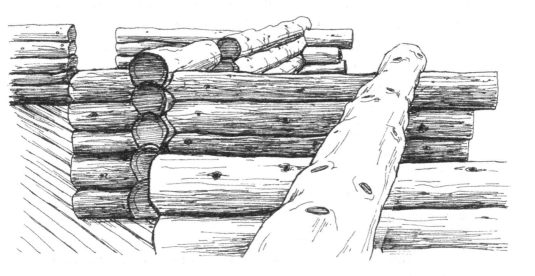

"Building this house has to make us better parents," I say to Todd, as I kick sand with my big toes. Sandpipers run a mile a minute, keeping their downy bodies two inches from the approaching water.

"How so?" he asks.

"On the building site, we confront problems every day," I explain. "We are forced to work together and solve them. Problem solving is what this building is all about: how to move logs, how to put them up, and how to bring them down, and do so quickly, safely, and efficiently. We are learning to work together. This discussing, this learning to read each other and know each other's personality, can only put our minds in touch and keep our avenues of communication open when it comes to raising our children."

"It's nice to know some good may come out of our struggle besides a warm house!" Todd replies.

When we return from the beach, our house of five rounds of logs has reached the height where windows will go. Todd is convinced that the log work will now become easier as the logs will be in smaller pieces and they should be easier to handle. But we are finding out quickly that that is not the case.

"It's falling!" he screams, as the log slides off the wall and into the foundation ditch. Up until now, when logs were long, we cranked one log end up and secured it on the building; and then fastened the rope on the other end that remained on the ground and cranked that end up. Shorter, dry logs were cranked up with the rope in the middle and raised in one attempt. Now the building is too high for that technique. Now the logs swing into a vertical position when we try to pick them up and then they fall.

"Watch out! It's falling again!" I scream, as we try to put the log up again.

"I'm so tired of it," Todd complains. "I'm ready to frame it out. I'm ready to saw those damn logs into boards." We pack up, angry at the log and at the derrick, and head home.

"It's stupid," Todd says, as he drives down the road, a little faster than usual. "Why would you want to put something up and knock it over, put something up and knock it over, while you're standing under it and it could kill you? You end up wrecking the building or wrecking your body, besides wasting a lot of time. This whole procedure is dangerous and stupid. We can't keep getting away with what we're doing and not get hurt."

If money were not an issue, we'd look for a secondhand crane or a backhoe to purchase to help us move the logs. Todd and I are doing the best that we can with our skill level and budget. But we must change it up when one method no longer works.

"The derrick is obsolete," Todd announces. "We used it for two rounds of logs and now it's useless. I really thought it was the ticket. Now all building *must* stop. I have to take all my time and energy and invent some new way to lift those logs. If someone would want to buy this house after it's complete, we'd probably never want to do it. But right now, if someone made an offer, I'd seriously think about it, and it wouldn't have to be too damn much!"

When some folks learn that we are building a log home, they invariably have a friend or a relative that built one, too. We usually have to ask, "It's probably a kit, right? Ours is from scratch." We feel so silly saying "built from scratch" as if we were making a cake. They ask us then if we are "skinning" our logs, as if they were rabbits or squirrels. And when we cut the horizontal groove in the log with the chain saw, are we "gutting" them?

Todd's cousin and her husband invite us to see the log house they are building from a kit in York County, Pennsylvania. We have never seen a log kit home up close and are very interested. We are amazed at what we find. It is a very handsome house, but we have difficulty calling it "log." The trees were milled into timbers, flattened on three sides and curved on one, in an attempt to resemble what it once was—a tree. All pieces are exactly the same, mass produced like telephone poles. Running your hand across the side of one, all you feel is smoothness and flatness. They are very narrow in width—eight inches—and can be carried under your arm. To Todd and me, a kit home feels like a stacked, milled timber home.

When you run your hand across our log walls, there are curves and bumps and bulges over knots where branches once extended. Each log is individual, and they still feel like trees. Some of our logs are eighteen inches wide, looking massive and sturdy and feeling it, too! A kit home *should* go up much easier and quicker. The struggles we are having suddenly seem a little more worth it to us. We really are getting something very beautiful and unique for our toil.

Todd now walks around totally immersed in thought. I can speak to him, right by his side, and he never hears me. The log-lifting problem has full control of his brain. Our last attempt to lift logs onto the building with the derrick made it crystal clear that he must now take the time out of building to design and build our skyline before we can proceed. Sooner or later we knew it would come to this. Two large oak trees positioned on either side of our house are one of the reasons this particular site was chosen. We got a ¾-inch cable from Demolition King Uncle Iggie that will stretch across our building thirty feet in the air and act as a skyline. To get it up to that height, Todd nails narrow strips of wood onto the two large oak trees that are on either side of our building, to act as a ladder. The hard oak resists every blow of the hammer as he nails in the ladder rungs. This is exhausting and frightening work twenty-five feet in the air.

Once Todd hauls the cable up, stretches it above and across the building, and fastens it to the two trees, we decide the cable can do double duty. We can suspend two huge thirty-by-fifty-foot plastic tarps that we purchased and hang them from the skyline cable to cover and protect the log building from the elements. Since our first truckload of logs sat for so long before we began to build, we have some rot on those bottom three rounds. The quicker the building gets covered, the less wood we will lose. The tarps seem to be the answer.

Todd slips S-hooks into the tarp's grommets and slides one of the curves of the S over the cable like a giant shower curtain. One tarp will cover the north side of the building, the other tarp the south side. I unroll and loosen the tarps as he pulls them skyward to the cable. The first problem is that the grommets are not attached at the same exact distance apart on both tarps, thereby preventing both tarps from lining up at the same hook. The second problem is that as Todd hangs the tarp, hook by hook, the weight causes the tarp still on the ground to twist and bind. His right hand squeezes each S-hook closed to prevent them from opening up, while his left hand hangs on to the tree for dear life. I pull on the rope attached to the far end of the tarp and yank it across the building as he hooks up length after length.

Todd's face looks mighty upset. Grommets are ripping out left and right. He's extremely tired from holding himself up, and his hand aches

from squeezing the metal hooks closed. The wind gets trapped under the plastic and moves the tarp wherever it pleases. It gets hung up on the log walls and down in the cavity where the cellar steps will go. I run around the floor of the building trying to loosen the tarps free. The wind fills the plastic and pushes me toward the cellar step cavity with such powerful force that I struggle to remain upright.

When Todd is finished hanging the tarps, he descends the ladder and we look the situation over. The size of these tarps is extraordinary, blowing and pushing, rising and falling like great sails on a ship. We each take the end of a rope that's attached on the tarp's lower corners and try to pull the ends out, over the building. We try to tighten them and secure them like a taut tent, but we have no control.

We work at it for an hour until Todd ascends the ladder once more and takes down the tarps, S-hook by S-hook. His face is not upset anymore, but totally hopeless and defeated. We fold up the monsters and drive home in silence.

Back home, while Todd washes the dishes, I record in my journal and try to get him to tell me how he feels about the whole thing.

"Tell me about today and the tarps." He shakes his head no.

"You don't want to talk about it?" I ask again. His head shakes no again.

"I want to find a way to *stop* thinking about it," he replies. "I felt real foolish standing up there, especially after I realized it wasn't going to work. I couldn't talk myself into believing that it would. The size of those tarps was tremendous, bigger than a sail on a boat. Hell, you could jump out of an airplane with it. I've never, ever seen anything like it on any building site. They're not made to hang or be in the air where they can catch wind. They're for covering dirt piles or something."

He picks up the catalog that we ordered them from. "Here's a picture of one over a camper trailer. *That's* what they're for. I just don't want the house to rot, honey. I don't want the tarps to rip. I don't want any more headaches, and I don't want it to be hard to get the logs up anymore."

"The skyline should take care of that," I say.

"If I can get it to lift up a log. That's another story. All these log building books say you can use anything to lift a log—a truck, horse, winch, a come-along, but they left out one thing—how to do it."

We manage to lift a log by attaching a locking block and tackle to the cable. We pull on the rope together under the suspended log and yank it into the air. The only problem is the two oak trees that the cable is attached to bend and sway with every pull. There are also dead branches in the two oaks, and we imagine them breaking free and falling on us. Our hard hats wouldn't do much good because we have to bend our heads way back and look up to watch the log. Now we have a new challenge: take the tops off the two oak trees so we can utilize the skyline cable most efficiently.

Todd announces he is going to take care of topping the trees the next day while I am away at work.

"Without spiked boots, without a climbing harness, without the knowledge of how to perform tree surgery, and without someone on the ground to rush you to the hospital if you fall or cut yourself. Sorry. Case closed," I say. In the meantime, our friend Mick, who was once a tree surgeon, informs us that he can borrow the proper safety equipment and will do it for us the next chance he gets. Until then, we can only put logs on the building when someone comes to help.

Fortunately, the very next weekend Todd's entire family comes to help, grandparents and all. Three generations of men hop on a log and begin peeling, while the women sweep up the sawdust that's piled on the floor. "Looks like you didn't clean up since we were here last, two months ago," my mother-in-law comments, laughing.

"That's only one day's sawdust, Mom," I reply.

Every time we roll a log over on the building, Grandpa Linch yells, "Ouch! My fingers!" When Todd's stout Grandma Linch sweeps close to the cellar steps hole, Grandpa yells, "Get away from there! You'll fall in there and we'll never get you out."

"The crane's right here," she replies, laughing. "You could pull me out with the derrick!" I bring out a bag of gingersnap cookies and although no one is hungry, Grandpa takes three. In a few minutes he's back. "Where's that bag?" he asks. "Someone must have stolen them out of my pocket. They're gone!"

Hard work mixed with good-natured fun makes log building a joy. Before the day is over, we have a half a round of logs peeled, up on the building, and notched down. It only takes one day of work for helpers to realize the magnitude of this project, how very many steps go into each log, how long it all takes, and the skill required to perform many of the tasks. When they see how difficult it is for a team of workers to manage just one log, they have a hard time comprehending how Todd and I can get anything done alone.

Just like my grandmother, Todd's grandmother shakes her head and says, "Youse work too hard. Too much work," in her strong Pennsylvania German accent. The day's end finds Todd and I feeling very warm inside. "I really enjoy working with people that I love," he says. "Everyone has this common goal. They're not trying to build our entire house but just do a good job that day. They ask questions, come for help, fetch things for each other.

"When my family is all together, they don't talk much, especially about things that are important, but they are good workers. When you work together, you are exposed to the same elements. You all get tired or cold or hungry together. And at the end of the day, you all step back and see how much got accomplished and can all feel good about it. But most importantly, by them coming to help, it's like saying, 'We believe in your dream, want to share in it, and help you turn it into reality.' That's one of the best things anyone could do for us."

The tables are turned today. The oak skyline trees are being topped and Mick is in charge of the project. He gives Todd orders instead of the other way around. Climbing makes Mick nervous, but once he's up, his confidence and his knowledge return. He remembers how to tie certain knots and how to work the pole to get his rope around limbs. He ties his harness to two limbs in case he accidentally cuts the one that's holding him up in the tree and leans back in the air until the rope grows taut and holds him. Another rope, looped over the limb he's cutting, goes down to the ground to Todd and me. We pull on it so each of the branches will fall in a particular—and safe—direction. Our log building is on one side of the oak tree and the slate roof is piled on the other, not a large margin for error.

It's very, very cold this early December morning. Todd and I shiver down on the ground, awaiting commands, while Mick sweats and strains in the tree. He leans his back into the Y in the tree, his threadbare cotton jeans showing his underwear beneath, and takes a cigarette break. We send up a drink of water in a plastic cup on his rope, never spilling a drop. We had acquired a very small chainsaw from a lady friend whose husband left her and his tools behind. It comes in handy for Mick's one-handed cuts high in the tree.

Topping the first tree takes many more hours than Mick anticipated. When he descends to earth, I try to feed him the lunch that he missed hours ago.

"Can't eat," he says. "I'm having an adrenaline rush. I feel really worked up, like I just stepped off of a roller coaster, like chemicals are surging through my body." He was calm up there but now that he's down on earth, his brain is realizing where his body has been and it's catching up.

After a break, Mick goes on to top the second oak tree. As the day burns away, our two oak trees go from full limbed spreads that bend and sway in the wind to two rooted poles that move no more. Todd has had a smile on his face all day long. He's happy the job is being done right and is grateful for Mick's help. We are one step closer to a better way of lifting logs.

THE NEW LOGS

New logs are coming tomorrow. Truckload #3. To get ready, we are moving our remaining logs from the last load back to our designated septic area to set up for winter peeling. Usually we can only manage to move one or two a day, but today, we're shooting for six.

Todd and I maneuver a log off the pile and onto the wheels. The logs are long, and we must gather speed to take them back from the edge of the field where they were dumped and get up the slight incline on the driveway back to the building. As soon as we hit the grade it stops us, poised, motionless, but straining nonetheless attempting to move. The wooden timber carrier handle buries deep in our guts as we bend over pushing. One leg is forward on tiptoe. We teeter between drifting backward or continuing forward. Seconds pass. Muscles strain. Heartbeats speed up. We finally get the wheels and the log to move forward, ever so slowly. "Don't lose it! Keep going!" We push the log up to the flat. I lower my handle and collapse on the log, panting—hands aching where my callouses grip the handle. Every time, it feels as if we are running a sprint.

Next, we must push the log into our septic area, which has matted down hay two feet deep. Pushing the tires through it is like plowing. After moving six logs back, we are beat and can work no more.

When Randy unloads his truckload of logs the next day, he asks if we want them any particular place. He brings six more back to the building site in a snap. Puts four in our parking area and multiple logs in the field next to the pile. This is to prevent them from freezing in a mass once the snows arrive. If we can't lay logs on the building, we can peel these all winter long and lay them down like crazy come spring. The whole idea is to just keep making progress.

HINTS & TIPS:

- As far as positioning logs on your building: if you have a concrete slab, using a huge derrick with considerable weight on it to counterbalance would enable you to move your logs and work on them. A gin pole, which is basically a hand-built crane with a boom and a winch attached, is also a very effective method of moving and positioning logs. If it is set up right, the pole can swing a log from the log pile to the building and then down again for carving and sawing.

- One of the biggest things we would do differently if we had to build again is invest the time and money into a better, more effective log moving system. A gin pole would be our first consideration but it would still be a huge undertaking as you must take a massive tree and instead of cutting it down, it would be like putting a tree up, planting it. You would need to get ropes high up in nearby trees, anchor the bottom, and lift it up at two different points, but it would work magnificently.
- Exercise extreme safety measures at all time. We were very fortunate not to have a single accident on our building site and never even required a Band-Aid. Others might not be so lucky. Don't take chances.
- Every single person has a different level of strength and stamina. No two are alike. No one should ever be made to feel like a slacker if they grow more fatigued before another. Honor where your body is, knowing its strength will increase in time and with work. If others don't honor it, take care of your own needs.
- Sharing an experience like a day or weekend of work on your dream home with your extended family can create a lasting memory. If they don't offer themselves, ask and plan a work trip, making sure there is fun involved and you are not a hard taskmaster. Good chance they may return for another! Feed them well.

10
Another Hard Winter

THERE ISN'T MUCH MOVEMENT THIS winter. The month of December was consumed by making Christmas presents, and afterward, it's difficult to resume. The only forward movement we've made is up and down our icy driveway. When Todd has the truck all loaded, raindrops

begin to ping on the hood and windshield. We climb into the cab anyway, ignoring them. He takes the turn from the highway onto our lane a bit too fast if he's going to be stopping to put on chains. "Aren't you going to put them on?" I ask, for a good portion of our driveway is on a north-facing slope and the cold and snow remain long after the sun melts it other places. "Takes too much time," is his answer.

We make it halfway up our half-mile drive when the truck comes to a complete standstill and spins in place on the ice. When Todd tries to back down, the rear of the truck slides toward the slope. He stops the truck and we get out to look the situation over. "What do we do now?" he asks. I am irritated that he didn't take the time to put chains on to begin with.

"Throw cinders under the back tires and try to go forward to straighten out," I suggest. It works. Todd gets out the chains and is ready to lay them under the wheels when the truck begins to drift backward into Todd! I look at Todd, panic stricken, and then the truck. The emergency brake is on but it's not holding! Todd throws out his arms and tries to hold back the truck with his body. He slides backward on the ice and could easily fall and go under the tire!

"*Get in!*" he yells, as it moves by me. "Get in?" I ask myself. And go along *with it,* as it slides out of control? Try to steer it down the icy hill and go off the side with it? I don't like that idea. Suddenly the truck stops moving. We are both shaken. Todd stands upright from behind the truck and peers around to the side, trying to determine what magically stopped it. The front door on the driver's side, which Todd had left open, is jammed into the earth on the upper slope of the road. That's all that's holding the truck up! "It could rip the door off!" Todd exclaims.

Todd grabs the chains and lays them under the wheels and then hops into the driver's seat. I go up on the bank with the peavey and knock the dirt away from the door ever so slowly. The truck slowly rolls back onto the chains and stops. Todd hooks the chains, climbs into the driver's seat and inches back down the icy road, hitting the brake every few seconds. But, as the left rear tire rolls, its chain keeps sliding off.

Should I tell him and upset him more, or hope it hangs on until the end? It's doing *some* good half on. I let it go. When we finally get down to the flat, it is raining hard.

One of the chains gets stuck as Todd is taking them off and he has to take a deep breath and stick his head under the truck, right in front of the exhaust pipe to work on it. His face is purple when he pulls the chain out. "Let's go the hell home," he says.

"Look at the bright side," I tell him, on the way home over the mountain. "No one got hurt. The truck didn't hit any trees nor go over the bank. Where's your sense of humor?"

"That went a long time ago," he says. Don't I know it.

Throughout the month of January, we make three more attempts to peel but spend our day on the icy road instead, backing down without chains. As the Pennsylvania Germans say, "We grow too soon old, and too late smart!"

It's just as well with me, this no work. It's wicked cold outside now. Five degrees and high winds. It feels like we live on the Canadian tundra. When we do make it up to the building site, Todd spends a great deal of time in the air in his trees adjusting the skyline. I stand below on the ground freezing, waiting to fetch him things, with a cramp in my neck from looking up. Our house that we live in now doesn't feel much warmer. The loose windowsills rattle. The many panes of floating glass in the sash windows that cover the house on all four sides are in dire need of glazing. We're not home long enough to keep our woodstove going. The firebox is small in the cookstove, and the fire goes out in a few hours.

All night long the house grows colder and when we're gone all day, no heat gets pumped into it at all. The water in my pee bucket freezes overnight in our bedroom. We sleep with the electric blanket on all night long, *and* an electric bed warmer under our mattress, *and* cover with a down comforter. We eat our meals positioned right in front of the cookstove when it's this cold. In fact, we do countless activities by it. I pull the phone cord over when it rings. I take the rocker over when I write and put my feet *inside* the oven. When I type at my desk, I wrap a wool blanket around my legs, wear down booties on my feet, and sip cup after cup of hot tea to keep my fingers warm. Typing is hell with cold hands.

Todd came home from work tonight and told me there is a chance that he could get laid off. That means full-time work on the house in the winter. Joy! Last year I managed to get pneumonia and got out of work for two to three months. "What can I do this year?" I ask Todd jokingly. "Injure myself?"

"You'd better not," he says.

When we go up to the land, our work is really hindered by the weather. Scribing a notch is very difficult because although we brush the snow off the top of the logs with a broom, the sun melts what we miss and runs the water down underneath, where it freezes. Ice is impossible to scribe over.

Todd is not comfortable working on icy logs. He stands upright on the slippery logs and announces, "I don't like this at all. This ice really scares me." Besides the icy conditions, Todd has a big problem on his mind—our roof design. It needs to be totally revamped. He doesn't know how many rounds of logs we have yet to go. We can't put the roof design off. It's going to take him days to figure it out. "I didn't want to come today," he announces from up on the building.

The log truss design we originally chose to use in our building has a horizontal collar tie partway up the triangle, which adds support. The truss would sit on knee walls, three or four more rounds of logs after the second floor, which would enable us to gain some headroom. But that particular truss design would end up putting the collar tie at chest height on the upstairs living space and prevent us from walking back and forth across the room. The pitch of our roof and the truss design, therefore, needs to change and get very steep, and push the collar tie of the truss higher in the ceiling in a narrower triangle, so that there is enough headroom to walk under it, and eliminate the knee walls.

"Let's pack it up and go home," I advise. "No sense our bodies being here if our minds are not."

Todd made a model of our home out of one-inch wooden dowels so he could visualize what he has to do in real life. Reading a blueprint doesn't quite cut it in Todd's brain, especially our scrap paper drawings, and he does much better with three dimensions than two. He feels he must rip apart the wooden model and get the roof system straight before he can put one more log on the actual building. Tonight, on the floor, by the kerosene heater, with his rump in the air, Todd tears his model apart. Piles of logs with dried glue marks at previous notches litter the grass-colored living room rug. He uses a coping saw to cut new notches and redesigns the truss system.

"I'm going to burn this when the log work is done in the first fire we make in our new home," Todd says.

"*No!* Keep it for our children's Christmas train platform."

That model solved more than one problem and settled more than one argument. For example, when we designed the porch off our bedroom, Todd wanted to carve a hallway out of our room on a sharp angle so traffic wouldn't have to go right through our bedroom to reach the porch. "There won't be any room left for a dresser or a bureau," I say, "let alone a double bed!" To settle the disagreement, Todd made a wooden bed out of a block of wood to scale and couldn't even get it into the strange triangular shaped room. "Forget it!"

After a few weeks of staying indoors, me writing and Todd working in his woodworking workshop (that he purchased with my secret money), cabin fever descends upon us. "Let's try to go up and work," I say. This time we get smart and leave the truck at the bottom of our hill. We load up our two plastic kiddie sleds that we bought to haul tools at log

building school and pull them up our steep power line. The snow is deep, but we don't sink in for there is a thick, icy crust on the surface. No one comes to help in the winter, and I can't say that I blame them. As a result, Todd and I enjoy being together and iron out some of the kinks in our working relationship.

Before we begin a new round of logs, Todd goes around to all of the last notches on the building and measures their height to determine how thick the next log must be to properly fit over it. He figures and reads the measuring tape; I act as his secretary, recording. When we are finished, I have numbers for about seven logs—their length and the thickness each butt and top must be. Out at the log pile I walk back and forth eyeing up the pile. "What is the diameter of this log?" I ask. "How much length can I get out of it before it bells or twists? Go fifteen feet and tell me the diameter. Can I get a twelve-footer out of it? No, too skinny. How about a ten-footer? Next, I need a six-footer that has an eleven-inch top." Todd hops around the logs with his logger's tape and his red lumber crayon to draw cut marks. He didn't always trust me like this. He needed to see the list. He didn't like relying on me to tell him what we needed. He would get confused and say, "I can't tell what I have."

"Never mind, just cut. I know what we have." Sometimes he checks on me and says, "We already have an eight-footer cut."

"We need two," I reassure him.

It's taking some time, but we are settling into our individual jobs and do work rather well together. But every now and then we have a relapse. Today we have to unroll a log on the wall and Todd was thinking out loud how to set up the scaffolding to cut it.

I suggest a certain way, but he doesn't hear me. I can tell because he has a faraway look in his eyes as I speak to him. He's working a different idea out in his own head. I don't push mine. His setup does not work, however, so he must start over and come up with a new plan. Piece by piece, he moves things into the exact scaffolding design that I told him about earlier, which he never heard. Every step makes me laugh and shake my head more. He doesn't believe me when I tell him that I planned that, too. I don't always get much credit when it comes to figuring. "I don't feel sorry for you one bit having to move those big heavy planks," I tease him.

These days, a lot of time must go into rigging up scaffolding to work on our logs. We used to bring them back down to our subfloor to cut and finish but at round eight, we're quite high above the floor and it involves too much work and energy to lift and lower. "When I stood on the floor to cut, it's solid and secure," Todd says. "I knew the log wouldn't move. That's not the case anymore."

Cement blocks wobble on top of uneven oak planks that serves as a subfloor. Then sawhorses go on top of them, then more planks, then log stumps (of various heights), and then even more planks. "I must constantly tell myself over and over in my head, 'Don't move your feet. Don't move your feet.'" Todd says. "I can't ever be *not* thinking about it for one second. One half step to the side and I will fall and

break my neck. It's good that I don't have to concentrate very hard on cutting anymore. I need all of my mental energy to remind myself not to move."

It's pretty scary up there and really hard on Todd's back. He doesn't have as much freedom to move and must hold his body and his muscles in certain rigid positions to execute his cuts. "I used to be excited about cutting notches," Todd says. "I used to think, all right! Two notches to cut, and really get into carving because it was such a cool thing to do. Now, I think, '*Shit!* A notch! *Shit!* A flyway! *Good!* A lateral groove, they're easy and quick.'"

"Are you disappointed in me for not getting really good and fast at cutting notches so I could relieve you?" I ask.

"No," he says. "You wouldn't like working on those heights at all and your back would really kill you." My modeling for life drawing class is taking its toll on my posture and back.

Too many sitting positions with no support.

"You'd never be as fast," Todd adds. "My saw cuts so much quicker than your saw but it is way too heavy for you. It's even heavy for me. The jobs you do are important, honey. You're really good at what you do."

My face looks sad. My poor husband gets all the lousy jobs, all the strenuous, scary, and stinky exhaust-fume-inhaling cutting jobs. But how I appreciate him!

Eight rounds complete. With our new roof design, we've cut three rounds of logs out of our workload. That's thirty-nine logs! We figure only four more rounds to go and then the trusses. It will soon be a year and a half that we've been working on our home. The project has begun to wear us down. But then again, it's winter. Winter makes me feel old because it's something that I dread, and every year it gets harder to live this kind of minimalistic lifestyle in an uninsulated house. But today, while we work high above the ground, straddling logs and working the wood with our hand tools, the first flock of geese flies over. We both stop scraping, our tools fall silent, and we raise our eyes to that magical sound that fills the air. Their honking lifts our spirits and fills our eyes with tears. "First sign of spring, honey," I tell Todd. "The end is almost here."

HINTS & TIPS:

- Safety when working high on the building is extremely important. Your comfort level will depend on if you are used to heights, have good balance, etc. We used a combination of pallets, planks, sawhorses, blocks, and chains to accommodate our ever-changing needs for scaffolding. We spent a lot of time setting up scaffolding, and although it wasn't the safest method, we were fortunate not to suffer any mishaps. On the other hand, securing reliable, safe and sturdy scaffolding ahead of time is worth it. Used scaffolding might be available from retiring contractors or house painters. It is the type of thing that you ought to be able to sell once you are done with building your log cabin.

- If you have a good solid floor, you could rig up safer and more secure scaffolding. Doing all your cutting on the ground or on the building's floor is much safer than doing it ten feet high on the building.
- Working through the winter on your log building can be extremely challenging if you live in the colder climates. Everything takes longer, and it is harder to accomplish tasks. There is the added danger of ice when maneuvering on the building. Cut yourself some slack. Consider taking some time off if you're able during the harshest weather. If you fall ill because you are pushing too hard and not taking care of your health, your body will rebel and grow sick and then you will be taking time off anyway, so work smarter.

11
Help Arrives

MICK IS STARTING TO FEEL confident with the log work. Since the weather has broken, he's been helping on weekends regularly. He's getting the hang of our techniques and procedures and is particularly fond of moving logs—his favorite—for he can use his massive strength. And because of it, Mick seems to have replaced me as Todd's assistant. They put their heads together and devise ways to move the logs. When I open my mouth with a suggestion, it seems to fall on deaf ears. Even Todd seems to keep me on the periphery, which is unusual. There are no touches of affection as he passes by, as there are when we're alone.

I feel like the hired hand. Most of the day I stand in the shadows, waiting to fetch. Mick is much stronger than me, so when he's around I bow out gracefully as Todd's right-hand worker, but what I can't handle is my voice disappearing from the building scene altogether.

"*Get away from that log!*" Mick screams to me often. He is very jumpy when he's under a suspended log, but Todd and I have grown comfortable with big heavy logs dangling overhead. Mick instructs me to loosen the rope that is laced around the nailed boards on the skyline tree so the log can be pulled down the cable. When I get over to the tree, he forgets his initial order and yells, "*Get away from there!*" Logs don't usually just fall, and even if this one did, the tree is between me and the suspended log. "You just told me to loosen it," I reply.

"Oh," he says sheepishly.

A few minutes later, the three of us are discussing our next step and Mick says, "*She* can do that."

"*She!*" I blurt out. "*She* has a name!" Smoke is coming out of my ears. I avoid Mick for the rest of the day. I am stunned at this treatment, for Todd and I have never had issues over gender. He has always treated me as an equal whether it was on our long trail adventures, in normal life, or on the building site. He may have carried more weight in his backpack than me as his body is bigger and stronger, and he may do more strenuous jobs here at the building site for the same reasons, but we *both* do important and valuable work and each do our share, one unable to accomplish much without the other's contribution. We are both equally essential, just as it is in our marriage and how it will be raising a family together.

Later that afternoon, as we're peeling logs, Mick says to me, "You got awful quiet awful fast." I am shocked he even noticed.

"I didn't like the way you yelled at me," I tell him.

"I'm really paranoid about logs hanging overhead," he says.

"You *never* talk to Todd that way."

"You're a woman," is his reply. Should I feel complimented or insulted?

"This is the second time I got mad at you," I announce. "The first time was when we were laying the subfloor and you didn't want to work with me."

"I don't remember that." He wouldn't. I kept my hurt to myself and retreated quietly to the truck cab, teary-eyed. This time I needed to confront him. Being passive is not the answer. It's best to bring things into the open instead of harboring ill feelings.

After a while he says, "If you only get mad at me two times in two years, that's not so bad."

"No, I guess not," I say smiling. Before too long, Mick asks if I want to shoot his muzzleloader. He brings it up to play with when the log work is slow and there are few jobs for him. "No, I don't think so." Then I reconsider. He's reaching out to me. I better meet him halfway.

His new sensitivity warms me. Sharing my feelings was all it took to change our treatment of one another. From then on, things are fine between us.

Working with helpers can be hard on Todd, too. Delegating authority is not his forte. Our friends yell, "Give me a job! I'm here to work!" No one likes to sit around. Keeping the work flowing is fatiguing. All Todd can do is cut, cut, cut. All other jobs depend on his progress. So, I'm the delegator. I run around and watch everyone, giving advice here, showing someone timesaving tricks there. When we give someone a new job, we must first teach them, then we must watch them, then tell them tips and time-savers, then tell them how to fix their mistakes, or even do it ourselves. Todd instructs me, "Stay with him." He trusts people's skill less than I do. He wants things done right or he'd rather do *everything* himself. He's a tough one. But when it comes to moving tonnage, these strong, able bodies wouldn't be exchanged for all the skill in the world.

A new helper has arrived on the building scene, Russell Raeder, a coworker of our neighbor, who is considering building a log home for his own family someday. What better way to help make that decision than to work on someone else's home first?

Russell is another big boy like Mick, but his strength isn't so obvious. It's hidden. Actually, I think it's in the form of determination and a desire to please. When you say you need a tool, Russell *runs* to get it. When I go to climb our rickety ladder, he runs over to hold it steady. When he's asked to pull the skyline rope, he jumps off the ground, grabs hold of the rope, and hangs on in the air! He is so enthusiastic and pulls so fast and hard that the log bounces and jostles in the air when he's done with it. When you say, "Thank you, Russell," he replies, "Thank you!" and tips his baseball hat. His face is young and boyish and breaks out in a grin often. He makes us scratch our heads and wonder why. Who is doing whom the favor? But Russell assures us he absolutely loves log work.

Our helpers have to possess some kind of love for Todd and me or the log work itself, because conditions on the site aren't the finest for our workers. Often people arrive to help unannounced and often without a lunch. I try to pack extras like peanut butter and crackers. Our regular fare like tofu spread on pita and three-bean salad doesn't suit these men's palates, especially Mick's. He's strictly a meat and potatoes man. He learned a long time ago to bring his own "meat sandwich" in a brown sack when he comes to help. "Roast beast on white bread. Hold the onion, lettuce, tomato, mayonnaise, mustard, and butter."

He does like his creme-filled cupcakes and Pepsi, however. When we know ahead of time that Mick is coming, we bring our three-gallon insulated water container, especially if it's hot and we're going to be peeling. Mick drinks huge quantities. We often forget cups. Then you have to set the cooler on the edge of the truck's tailgate, crawl underneath on the ground, and let the liquid fall into your mouth. Todd and Mick hold it one handed over their heads and let it arch into their opened lips, a difficult feat when it's full. We all avoid touching the nozzle because it's filthy and there never seems to be any time for cleaning.

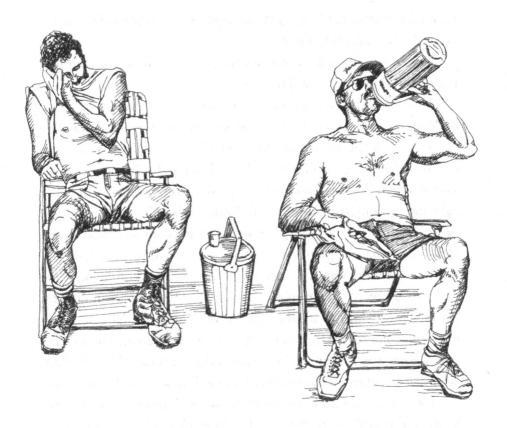

"Facilities" are at the end of a short trail leading back to a three-inch sapling that Todd placed horizontally in the crook of two trees as a seat, a few feet off the ground. The hole that he dug directly underneath the sapling fills up quickly as the soil is rocky and he couldn't dig it very deep. It's turning into a mound instead, with leaves piled in between layers and on top. Often, yesterday's deposit is gone when you go back the next day. (The neighbor's dog stops by regularly.) Now when Todd goes to relieve himself, he says, "Gonna go feed the dog."

In spite of the primitive conditions, our weekend help is frequent, and we cruise right into spring, our logs steadily disappearing from the pile. When our logger Randy, delivered our third load in November, we told him we would be needing one more load. We wanted them cut by winter, but they didn't need to be delivered until later if there was snow on the ground. Once again, we must listen to a myriad of excuses as to why he can't bring them.

Finally, he calls with an actual date. "Will you be at the land next Friday around suppertime? I'll bring them then."

At seven in the evening the next Friday, we wrap things up on the building and go out to the "shaving factory" to wait for Randy. We peel ever so slowly, for we are tired and have had a long day. We stop to watch the sun set behind the field of clover and then disappear. We stop to watch the deer come out of the bordering woods in the dusk light and we stop frequently to look down our lane for a logging truck. When it gets difficult to see, we decide to pack up and head home. Heavy hearted, we climb into the cab, meander down our lane and turn onto the highway. The cars have their headlights on by now and they pass us, piercing our vision. "Is that a logging truck?" Todd asks. My eyes focus slowly with the little bit of light that is left. Boom on top. Faint color red on the cab like Randy's truck. We watch in disbelief as he passes, crawling up the hill at five miles per hour. It's nearly dark. We make a U-turn on the highway and head back to the building site.

The logs hang fifteen feet beyond his rear bumper, cover his taillights, and nearly scrape the asphalt. His truck can barely move from the load. Finally, at the top of the hill, Randy grinds it into park, pulls on the air brakes, and jumps out of the cab.

"What, are you quitting work already? You still have an hour or so of daylight," he laughs. His sense of humor seems to be intact. "You wouldn't believe what it took to get this load here. I got payback for jerking you guys around so much. While I skidded your trees out this afternoon, a sapling hit me in the face and cut my nose and broke my glasses. Ripped the skin right off my hands." We look down, and sure enough, his knuckles look like hamburger, red and fleshy and shiny where they had been sprayed with first aid blood-clotting spray to stop the bleeding.

He continues. "I rushed home at 5:30. My wife quickly dug out another pair of glasses. I didn't take time to eat. Just grabbed two leftover Easter eggs out of my kids' nest."

"You're probably glad this is over, and you don't have to deal with us anymore."

"I don't really mind," he says. "You folks seem like nice people. If youse were jerks, I might feel that way."

By now, night has fallen. Randy climbs on top of his crane and asks Todd to aim our truck headlights onto the pile to help him see. Our sinister, electric line lurks close to his truck, ready to fry his brains if he touches it with the boom claw. Randy's silver hard hat glints in the light. Todd and I link arms watching the headlights illuminating the edges of the logs. He hugs me and we smile. "This is it, honey," he says. "The last of them. When these logs go, there won't be any more coming." It's a nice feeling.

Then he voices what we are both thinking. "They look really big. They look really heavy." Some old thirty-footers from the previous batch stick out of the pile and these new logs stick out ten feet further. "The truck's not going to be able to pull them off the pile. It can barely pull a thirty-footer off now."

The boom arm works and moves the log like it has a mind of its own. Logs bounce and settle in with a thud. Even in this dark hour, Randy spends a lot of time arranging the logs into a neat pile, straightening them so their ends are even, rearranging them so they fit neatly into spaces between logs. A few times he hits the steel side of his trailer with his boom arm when he swings a log around. He's trying to keep them low and duck beneath that wire. As he climbs down from the truck, I ask him if he's hungry.

"Oh, don't worry about it. I'll be okay."

"Take this sandwich. I made it for you," and I hand him a sandwich stuffed thick with peanut butter and jelly.

"Thanks a lot, I'm really starved," he says, taking the sandwich. "Heh!" he says to Todd. "Your wife's a good cook!"

I'm intrigued with this man and his line of work—the most dangerous occupation there is. It's a livelihood from centuries past. He works with such tonnage, such unpredictability, as he drives those grossly overloaded trucks, taking chances with his machines and the law. He lives on the edge. Feet propped up on truck bumpers, we chat as night falls.

I ask why the forest he's been cutting is being cleared. "I'm thinning rows in a pine plantation," he says. We're happy to think that we saved some trees from being turned into toilet paper. Todd and I are learning that Randy is really a nice guy. He didn't have to help us out. Cutting trees for pulpwood is Randy's livelihood and accommodating our unique needs for a log house was not profitable. In fact, he admitted that he ordinarily never works with individuals like us. We needed our logs at a certain time, and they needed to be cut a certain way. We put a lot of pressure on him, but we hadn't been aware of how we disrupted his regular work.

Todd and I run around the truck, directing Randy's rig backward. Our eyes are wide and glassy, alert like a wild animal's. Energized by the fact that this is our very last load of logs and acquiring them is over, we completely forget our past fatigue. We watch his rear lights fade down the road into the darkness, the truck rolling easily now that it's relieved of its load. Randy said we were welcome to stop by and see him anytime. He has become our friend. We said likewise.

HINTS & TIPS:

- Bear in mind that chainsaw work requires a high level of skill and is time consuming to learn and perfect. Do not allow casual visitors who come to help pick up a saw and with little or no practice, try to cut notches. Be careful who you allow to execute these important tasks, or they could destroy your logs.
- There is considerable physics involved with moving logs and a knowledge of using levers, fulcrums, and balance points is very helpful. You can learn as you go along, of course. If you know a log's balance point, you can move any size log by pushing, pivoting and rolling it. Tools like peaveys and wheels with a notched wooden axle can help logs move more easily once you locate their center of balance. These skills are more necessary if

you do not have a machine handy to move logs, but these tools and methods of moving will always be used on the building site.

- Have a collection of ropes, slings, chains, and pulleys available to move, pull, and position logs. If your building site is located on a hill, you will have more challenges using a machine.
- Bring extra food along to feed your helpers. Always pack extra when you're going to the work site for the day. Once word gets out that you are building, folks may start to come to lend a hand.

12
Full Time

SOME TIME AGO, I TOLD Todd about the secret bank account into which I'd been squirreling money so he could quit his factory job and build full-time, living on savings. That time has finally come. It's April and we'll be able to put in three packed months of heavy-duty building. Our goal is two rounds of logs a month, and the third month to build and put up our five massive log trusses that will support the roof. In June, with the log work hopefully complete, we'll cover up the building, no more to rot, and head for the high Sierra Nevada Range of California to hike eight hundred miles on the Pacific Crest Trail. The great planner, I am. The great goal setter. Problem is, if we don't accomplish our log building goals, I can easily adjust. Todd can't. Deadlines and schedules are written in stone in his brain and he works like a fanatic to meet them.

Nonetheless, he's happier now that log building is the only work responsibility in his life. It's only been a week since he quit his job to build full time and already he's said, "It's like I never worked at the kitchen cabinet factory. I hardly remember it. There's something else to take its place. Something better."

I, on the other hand, am having a hard time adjusting. When Todd went to work at three in the afternoon, my time was my own. For the last few years, I could go for a nice walk, visit a neighbor, talk on the phone, write in my journal, or do whatever I wanted. Now,

our workday on the house begins at 8:00 a.m. and ends at 8:00 p.m. There's supper to be made, lunch to prepare for the next day, and mail to sort and answer before collapsing into bed.

When my sister finally reaches Todd after having called the house day after day for weeks, she reprimands him, "Don't kill my sister."

"There's a certain amount of work that needs to get done," he tells her. "Whether we do it now or stretch it out, it still has to get done." There's that blasted schedule I made, and we have to stick to it!

We drive over the mountain to our land mostly in silence. I watch out my window for wild animals. We top the mountain and look out into the next county. Is it sunny? Look like rain? There are two distinct sets of weather on either side of this 1,500-foot mountain range. You'd think it was the Continental Divide. Once down the other side, I go back to my own window and he to his driving. He watches the curve of the road, looking for potholes, letting the big red truck roll a little too fast down the mountain. The line painters were just out. A dead groundhog lies in the way, painted right over his furry, stiff body. Two brilliant yellow stripes mark his bloated belly.

Once at the land and working, we each do our own jobs, moving smoothly through the motions we've grown so accustomed to. Todd talks to me little now. He doesn't comment when I make a statement. If I ask why, he says he didn't think it necessary. To answer even the simplest question like, "Are you hungry for lunch yet?" he must think for extremely long periods of time. His brain is overloaded. The building is growing and changing so quickly, he's having difficulty keeping up.

The number of things he must remember to do is very taxing: leave this log longer, curve this log here, flatten this one now, stop this wall here, extend this log here, etc. And, he's not used to being with me *all the time*. When he was working at the factory, more than half of his waking hours were his own to spend with his own private thoughts. He's the type of person that needs that. But that is no longer the case. Now, his lovely wife is always by his side, butting into his thoughts. If I'm in someone's company, I like to communicate, at least every now and then. To compromise, I bring my journal, writing papers, and sometimes even my portable typewriter to work on a story or on my upcoming book, *Journey on the Crest*. My deadline approaches so I must continue making progress. I work on the back of the truck's lowered tailgate and sit on a log stump and work until Todd calls for my help. Much of the time, he is cutting very high on the building and there isn't much for me to do.

Todd is happy that progress is being made, but his work is now very difficult and dangerous. He has determined an optimum distance that a log should be from his saw to make it safe and comfortable to cut. He cannot maintain that safe and comfortable distance so high on the building. He cannot straighten his back; he cannot rest his arms but must hold that heavy saw out in the air, to make delicate cuts. The logs are huge, and the notches are deep, taking longer to cut and

prolonging his misery. He strains to move scaffolding and planks by himself, balancing high on the logs, while I sit and write. There's no room for me up there and no job that I can do but I need to be close-by and available; if nothing else but to take his saw from him so he can use both hands to get down from those heights. A little resentment builds up on his part and I can't blame him.

He turns his saw off and flips his face shield up, catching a breath of fresh air instead of exhaust fumes. The mesh on his shield has a hole in it right where his long German nose sticks out from his face. The jagged wire cuts his skin every time he flips it down, irritating him.

"We'll never get done!" he complains. "No matter how hard 1 work, we never seem to move forward. And I'm the one who has to do most of the work."

"Don't resent me," I say. "Do you want to switch? Do you want to write this book? Everything evens out in life. Should I resent you when the baby cries in the middle of the night and I have to breastfeed? It will be my job. Why don't you come down and take a break?"

"*No!* I can't take breaks. The fuckin' house will never get done! How would you like to be up here busting your ass?"

"When I have to sit for half an hour in a modeling pose in life drawing class without moving and my back is killing me, should I resent you because you're not doing it? It's my job. Right now, it's your job to cut notches. You don't have to be happy about it. You can complain and bitch about it, but just because I am your wife and I am here, doesn't mean you can take it out on me."

I walk over to the log wall beneath him and take his monster chain saw from his hand. "Come and have a snack. I'll make you some peanut butter crackers." He sits down on the green and white webbed lawn chair and I go to sit on his lap. I pull up his shirt and tickle his hairy belly. I kiss his lips and smell bar oil on his face and exhaust on his breath. He smells and tastes like fumes.

"Depending on how my saw is tilted," he says, "I have to hold my breath it's so bad. If it's too long a time, I have to stop sawing and move it away just so I can breathe. My eyes burn. It's hell!" he says, with a small, little smile. "Some people go through life and never know what hard work is. Now that I know, I think I've had enough!"

The next morning, Todd goes over to our land early and I stay home to make a few phone calls. In the meantime, a census taker stops by to ask a few "work-related" questions.

"How many hours a week do you work?" he asks.

"About fifteen at the university," I say. (Not counting writing a book.)

"Why so few?" he asks.

"Because I don't want to work anymore."

"That's a good reason," the man replies. "A good enough reason. How about your husband? How many hours does he work a week?"

"None for pay."

"Is he looking for a job?" the man asks.

"No. We both work every day at building our house," I explain.

"That doesn't count. Only work for pay," the census taker clarifies.

What is the difference between working a job for money to pay someone else to build a home and building the house oneself, or working for money to buy food at the grocery and working at growing your own? It's all the same. It's all work. Many people in our society don't see it that way. For some reason, they think of us as lazy!

Log work continues at a steady, constant pace as the spring progresses and the days warm up. Outdoors nearly all of our daylight hours, we enjoy watching the trees leaf out along with other signs of the season. My thoughts of spring are mildly interrupted when I notice a few tiny

black bugs on the light-colored log that I'm working. They bore holes in the log the size of a pinhead and leave a small speck of sawdust behind. I crush them with my index finger and their remains are black and powdery, like charcoal. I don't pay them much mind.

The next day there a few dozen bugs and I go around to the top log, crushing them all and sticking my Swiss Army knife blade into their bore holes, hoping to kill them. The *next* day, there are hundreds and hundreds of them!

"Never mind," says Todd. "You're wasting your time."

"Where are they coming from?" I ask in amazement. "They weren't on the logs when we put them up. They must be coming out of the trees! "

Sure enough, our naturalist friend Tom Lecky says they are powder post beetles. May is their month to bore into wood and lay eggs. Later, they'll come out and die. The larvae, however, will stay in the log anywhere from three to twenty years, eating! The twenty-year eaters are called "death watch beetles." Tom has them in his house. They've been eating his floor and now he must replace it. We discuss fumigating at a later date but the thought of it makes Todd and me sick. It's just as depressing to think of our house being eaten before we even get a chance to live in it.

Like the bugs, our friends come out of the woodwork once again this spring, to help us meet our deadline. A new helper, another hiker, is on the scene, John Vincent from Massachusetts. He has come for a taste of log building, so we are making sure his mouth knows the flavor well before he leaves. We're working hard since John's been here and have finished the tenth round and pulled out the eleventh.

Our buddy Mick is here, too. He got mad at his boss and took a couple of sick days. The sun is wicked warm today and as usual, we're out at the "shaving factory," peeling. The guys take their shirts off while they work, and John reveals his white belly like a halibut and sunburned lines on his arms and neck. I cut my shirtsleeves off with Todd's pocketknife, and the neckband, too, to get some air down the front. Mick is into music and plays his "tunes" while we peel. He opens up the back hatch of his blue Dodge Omni and positions his moveable speakers to throw the music into the "shaving factory." Sporting dark glasses, the guys take a few minutes break and play their tools as if they're in a jazz band: strumming drawknives like guitars and blowing them like harmonicas, and plunking peaveys like a bass. "We be jamming," Mick says.

I've grown very fond of Mick and his silly expressions. "MO BACK!" he yells when he's instructing me to drive the truck backward to release the come-along rope, as we're raising a log on the skyline. He brings his muzzleloader up to the land to shoot at piles of old shingles and a bucket of leftover concrete as makeshift targets. "Gonna make *boom!*" he announces to Todd and me so we know to lower our ear protectors. He walks up to the ground behind his target and digs out the smashed, jagged lead. "Can you imagine that going into your body? It could wreck your day."

Sometimes he makes bombs with his black powder and uses his cigarette as a fuse to set it off, in an effort to entertain himself. He shares his Tastykake cupcakes with me, brings ice for our cooler, and asks if I like certain music when he plays for our peeling parties. He has a couple of hundred cassette tapes that he's recorded from albums. They're in a half dozen tape boxes that he carries in his car at all times, labeled very neatly. We know Mick is coming a half mile before he arrives, for his speakers are blaring out of his opened car windows as he drives up our shale driveway to the building site. The music helps the unpopular job of peeling go faster and the beat keeps our drawknives moving.

Today we're working the new batch of logs, the sappiest yet, and everyone is wearing "rag bag" clothes. I wear Todd's cutoff green Army fatigue shorts that are a bit too short. The sap sticks to the hair on my upper thighs, making it very painful to tear my bottom off the log when I must move to a new spot. I rub dirt onto the sap to take up the stick. Mick wears maroon polyester shorts. The waist is stretched out on them and he takes up the slack with a three-inch safety pin. Two big patches of sap coat his backside and make hundreds of pieces of sawdust stick to the fabric. He wears Pro Ked sneakers from K-Mart with big, white vinyl flaps over the laces like golf shoes. "What are they for?" I ask. "How should I know," he replies.

Todd wears his Chippewa black leather logging boots with his shorts. My husband has remarkably skinny ankles and draws the laces so tight that his feet look like Goofy the dog's, the Disney character.

When the tape ends, all at the "shaving factory" is quiet, except for the scraping of the bark. Todd is peeling at his one speed: top speed. I roll my back across the log and complain, "It hurts nearly all of the time that I peel."

"You need to do it more," he informs me. "You need to peel eight hours a day."

"I'd be happy if I never peeled again."

"Only two more rounds," Todd says. "You should cherish every stroke. After we're done, you'll probably come out here to peel old leftover logs just to reminisce."

"And you should cherish every notch you cut then, too."

Mick lights a cigarette and laying it on the log he is peeling gets up to flip the tape and get a drink. Fainter music from across the clover field wafts to our side. "Born to be WIIIIIIIILD! Born to be WIIIIIILD!" A doe comes out of the woods for a snack and lifts her head in that direction as if wondering what the noise is. It's the contractor working away on our neighbor's house. We hear staples being shot into the walls.

"We're losing the race!" Todd says. "Today the walls, tomorrow the roof. Strange, what it takes us a year to do they do in a day."

When we first bought our land there weren't any other houses on this whole ridge. Now one is up and two more are growing daily.

"We're making progress, too," I announce. "You can actually see our walls getting higher with all this help we've had." Today, besides Mick and John, Russell is here and it's a good thing because today, one of Todd's greatest fears comes true. The skyline breaks and a log falls on the building!

Since we have so much help, Todd decided to take advantage of the manpower and put the five, thirty-seven-foot logs on the building. The logs are lifted into the air by driving the truck down the lane, which pulls the rope of the locking block and tackle on the skyline, raising the log off the ground. Then we pull the suspended log above the building down to its designated spot. Since it's a locking block and tackle, someone has to stand directly under the suspended log to release the rope. The weight of a thirty-seven-footer makes it hard to lower the log slowly without having the rope yank out of your hands and send the log crashing onto the building. So, we decide to rig the truck up to the rope and let the truck release it instead of doing it manually. I am instructed to drive the truck forward just a wee bit to release the lock and then slowly back the truck toward the building, thereby easing the lowering log onto the building. Everyone knows their part. Russell and John are on ropes. Todd watches. Mick relays messages and I drive the truck. All systems are GO! and I begin to inch forward, waiting for the command to stop. I inch forward some more. No one yells. I look back and the log is already on the building, instead of in the air where I expect it to be. The spare link in the chain had broken where the skyline cable wrapped around the oak tree. "The weak link!" Todd yells, "If it was going to break, I knew it would happen there!" The log has fallen onto the building and is resting on the wall by only half an inch. Russell is shook. He was on the side where the log hit and thought it would hit him and go through the floor. No one was injured, thank God, not even the log.

Pulling straight down with all the weight of a thirty-seven-foot log was apparently too much stress on the cable. This log we managed to get down onto the building. How will we get the other eleven down?

"What we need is a skyhook," Mick says.

"Well, work is over for the day," the head log builder announces.

Over at the house, we swab ourselves with alcohol to get the sap off our skin. "I don't believe I'm making headway with this sap," Todd says. "I rub and rub and rub and sometimes I think I'm just spreading it around." While we rub, the men put on their thinking caps and try to figure out the skyline.

"How about if we just raise the log until it barely clears the building," Todd says. "When we move the log down the skyline, the cable should sag from the weight until the log is resting on the walls. If there's still too much tension on the locking block and tackle to release it, we can loosen the guylines that support the skyline trees to get even more of the log's weight onto the building. After that, we should be able to easily release it by hand."

What a wonderful idea! It should work great! That evening, after supper, we relax on the sofa and John begins to tell us what he has learned from log building.

"I never thought it would be so difficult. Peeling, I thought, was merely stripping bark off the tree, maybe smoothing it a little. I never thought about dealing with knots. I thought a drawknife was for decorative purposes. I learned a lot just by watching you both move your knives, the angles you approached the knots, and the pressure you applied. It's really an art."

John wasn't a good peeler when he first came to help us. I had a lot of his rough edges to clean up, but it was amazing how fast he progressed.

"I am also amazed how you can easily move tremendous weight by using a simple board as a lever and a log as a fulcrum," John continues. "What was most interesting though, was watching you, Todd and Cindy, interact. It was fun to listen to your conversation going back and forth when you disagreed on something. It always came back to your "mission" though. You are both working toward the same goal, so it doesn't make much sense to be at odds for very long. A strong foundation is certainly under your marriage, just like your house."

Listening to John share his thoughts makes Todd and I feel good inside. I go over and sit on my husband's lap and give him a big kiss. "Such a good log builder," I say, and rough up his full dark beard.

After John returns to Massachusetts, Todd and I are once again on our own, but with our new system of handling logs, we continue making good progress. On this particular day, I follow Todd to the land a little later and stop at the dairy for a surprise ice cream treat. When I pull up to the building, his head is sticking out of a window hole that he has just cut in the log wall, calling to me as if he were our future child, "'Hi Mama! I'm glad you're home.' Can you imagine, honey? Someday we'll hear that."

"Are you hungry?"

"No. I just ate a ton of peanut butter crackers."

"That's too bad. I bought you a treat." I make him close his eyes and open his mouth and slide a spoonful of mint chocolate chip ice cream into it.

"Ooooh!" He grabs the thermos and takes me around the house, showing me what he's done all morning. "I figured out the dimensions of our bedroom," he says. Strips of wood left over from cleaning out the inside of the log's groove are laid on the rough oak flooring, end to end in the shape of a rectangle. He throws himself into the corner and says, "Here's where the bed will go. Hop in! It's really starting to happen, honey. It's starting to look like a house. Come see."

We climb to the top of the dirt pile left by our excavator when he dug out the basement. The soil will be spread around the block wall later, when the electric is in and we need to backfill. We climb up here periodically for a bird's-eye view, mostly when another round of logs is finished so we can check our progress. The big thirty-seven-foot logs really make the building look different. It's beginning to look like a home that will soon have a roof and soon have people living in it. We sit down on top of the dirt and stones and get comfortable. "How was your morning?" Todd asks.

"Not very good. I talked with my mom on the phone before I came over. She isn't feeling well. She is tired and weak. She says she has this very sharp pain deep in the back of her chest. She's thinking of admitting herself to the hospital to find out what's wrong with her."

"You're kidding?"

"No. It really scares me. My sister JoAnn said she looks terrible, like Dad did right before he died." After a period of quiet, I say, just gazing at the house and thinking, "I don't feel much like building this afternoon. I'm feeling down."

"Why don't we just peel those two eight-footers that we'll use as upright posts in the sunroom and then call it a day."

After a few minutes peeling, I forget my troubles and get into the rhythm of the work. "Look here!" I call to Todd. "This log has two big brown knots on it the exact size and distance apart as two breasts and nipples would be. Let's carve a woman for the sun-room post!"

The next morning, we come to the building site prepared with woodworking chisels and mallets, life drawing and anatomy books, a book of Michelangelo's sculptures and a Playboy magazine for references. Todd makes me model—makes me lie on a sheet of plastic on the ground that's lined up to the log by my side. I take off my shirt and bra and raise my arms above my head while Todd takes a fat red lumber crayon and looks at my curves, lines, and hollows and draws them onto the smooth pine log. His eyes are quick and intent, like that of a draftsman, as he goes back and forth with his work.

Once he has the general shape, I get up and begin carving, too. I work on her breasts, carving areolae and raised nipples in the brown knots. Todd works on her thighs, hips, and belly. After we rough out her basic body lines, Todd starts the chainsaw to give us a head start. He cuts her waist in on either side but takes too much off her hips. "Cut it!" I yell. "She lost all her hips!"

We work away, carving separate body parts, with me having to stop every now and then by Todd's request, to lie down on the plastic sheet and act as a reference. "Let me work!" I say. "Look at yourself!" In a minute I turn around to see him with his pants down, pulling his genitals through his tightly closed thighs to see what a woman's groin looks like.

"What are you doing?" I laugh hysterically.

"I got tired of asking you to model."

When the day is over, we have an interesting log goddess to adorn our greenhouse, complete with back and buttocks in the rear view. We try to carve her facial features, but she ends up looking like she walked into a wall. As time goes by, the carved lady cracks where the wood is grooved—her hiney crack deepens and goes way up her back. Most people who come to visit thinks she looks great and adds a personal touch to our home. A few prudish people ask us if we're going to put clothes on her when our children grow old. I say, "This is art! I hope my son learns and respects the human body before he's sixteen and discovers it in the back seat of a car."

Memorial Day weekend rolls around, and I am not in a celebrating mood. I've been spending much of my time in the hospital while Todd has built alone. My mother has stopped eating, stopped drinking, and stopped communicating with us, her children. The doctors have performed a battery of tests and can't find anything wrong. All new tests have been put on hold until after the three-day weekend. My heart, once again, is not in my work. The big holiday weekend, I say to myself, "and where are we: Logland. Everyone is having barbecues and picnics and we're having sardine sandwiches for lunch. All Todd seems to need me for is moving an occasional ladder and handing an occasional wedge. I stretch out on a plank and try to cool off in the rising heat of the afternoon.

"I believe you're ready to quit!" Todd yells from the heights of the building.

"I just want to take a five-minute break. I'm hot. Is there something wrong with that?" I ask.

"I'll work myself if you feel sick. I feel wonderful."

"I'm glad."

"We never get anything done. We never come up here anymore and when we do, we make no progress!"

"I'm sorry my mom's in the hospital and maybe dying. I'm sorry she's a little more important than building."

"I believe you *are* ready to quit, aren't you?"

"And live in that drafty house the rest of my life? No! Can't I just take a lousy five-minute break?"

"I suppose you're not worried about this log at all. You're not worried how we're going to move it, are you?"

"Nope." I answer.

"Why not?" he asks.

"Because you'll figure it out."

"That's exactly the right answer," he says laughing. "Because I'll figure it out."

"You're the master log builder. Don't you want to be master log builder anymore?" I walk away smiling, and add, "I'm just along for the ride."

"Put *that* in your book!" he says.

After we finally get the gigantic log we're working on in place, Todd admits, "I'm sick of this. If I could be done with this, I'd be happy. I just want to get the thing done so I don't have to do it anymore."

Pushing to stay on schedule is taking its toll on him. Because of the hot weather, Todd's chainsaw heats up to point that it gets vapor lock and he can hear the gas boiling inside and it won't start. He stands up high on the building, pulling the saw's cord five, ten, fifteen times, and yells profanities—unusual for him but his ear protectors are on and he can't tell how loud his voice is. He has no patience for his saw running out of gas, either. It seems to run out of gas right before he's ready to complete a notch. He yells from the top log on the wall, "I should have a hose connected to a fifty-gallon drum of gas!" Actually, it's good it runs out as often as it does. He would never come down and take his much-needed breaks if it didn't. He stands by my lawn chair and pours himself a cup of water from the cooler, pretends he's going to drink it but spits the mouthful on my chest instead. "You said you were hot!" he yells, running away.

Later that day, the guys from the power company stop up to check on our neighbor's pole and come over to our place to see our progress.

"I'd like to see this place when it's done," one comments.

"I'd like to see it when it's done, too," replies Todd. "I'd like to see it done!"

Our departure date for our hike is speeding closer and we still have the rest of round eleven to put down, and all the trusses to peel, build, and raise. Todd is becoming very worried that we won't make our deadline. I'm beginning to wish I'd never set such a goal. (Of course, we could change our goal but not so easily done once cemented in Todd's mind.)

I understand his feelings. He wants to feel satisfied with the progress we've made on the house, be "deserving" of a long, three-month trip away from work. It would feel good to have all the logs peeled, the trusses built and raised, and the house covered with our big blue tarps. Then he could hike the Sierra with a clear conscience.

But things don't always work out according to plan. The unexpected can always happen. On June 7th, 1988, my mother has a massive heart attack in the middle of the night and stops living.

HINTS & TIPS:

- Be realistic about setting goals. Use them as a guide and as way to motivate but remain flexible if and when the unexpected in life occurs. Honor these unplanned for changes and have faith that the work on your home will be completed.
- If you are the type of person that benefits greatly from a break in your work and a change of scenery and pace, gift yourself that break. Chances are, you will return with renewed enthusiasm.
- Work on maintaining a sense of humor amid the seemingly endless and challenging work. It will enable you to persevere much longer and bring some fun to this big job.

13

Orphaned

I AM AN ORPHAN. THIRTY-TWO years old and no mother or father. My grandmother says not really, for I have a husband, yet I feel like one. Lately, I have little concept of the day, or week for that matter. I feel as though I'm living in some sort of limbo state. I feel numb, just filled with an overall feeling of remorse and utter sadness.

We're doing other things with our time besides building now. For one, the unsurmountable task of cleaning out my mother's home and getting ready to put it up for sale. Lots and lots of moving takes place—sofas, freezers, dining room sets are parceled out to my brothers and sisters. My mother had more sophisticated taste than I, so not many of her pieces go well in a log home.

No pink velvet chairs or Queen Anne end tables for us. We *will* take the washing machine, however. Our new log house will have plumbing someday and put an end to our seven-year lack. Since we are the only ones with a truck, we are transporting nearly every day, cranking up the mileage since my mother's house is thirty miles away.

We must also deal with thirty-five years of the accumulated material of a "saver." Together with my siblings, we divide articles into piles: yard sale, Goodwill, trash, and one for each of my mother's four children. It's very difficult to go through everything in the house and decide what is important enough to save, important enough to box it up, carry it home, store it, and then move it again when we move—things like the first drawings I ever made, and endearing cards we exchanged.

These are not things you should throw away. These things aren't "junk" or "clutter." It's what they are associated with that matters. Loved ones. Good times. Memories. Things that are a part of me and help make me who I am. Going through articles in my parents' house isn't causing me to live in the past. It gives me a firmer grip on the present. Knowing where I came from helps me to decide where I want to go.

My siblings and I take pieces of Mom's house to our own homes, into our own lives. We don't have our parents anymore in the physical sense, so we need the things that were closest to them. The things they used. The furniture they sat on. The paintings they looked at. We place them in our homes and hope to keep their memory alive.

In addition to moving out the contents of the house, we must get the house ready to sell. While the women go through drawers and boxes and wash floors and windows, the men paint walls, cut lawns, and trim hedges. The work lasts all through the month of June and into July. It's far different from how we used to spend our time. Todd and I neglected our families the past few years, while we spent every available minute up at our land building. When we began this project, we stopped spending Sundays with the family. We wouldn't miss more important events like birthday parties, but we often didn't arrive until after dark or after a full day's work was in. Just the opposite is true now. I am with my sister and brother nearly every day as it used to be when we were young and lived at home. In all the sadness we feel, this new closeness begins to make up for our loss.

As if dealing with my parents' house isn't enough to do, there is also the task of packing supplies for our three-month journey. Departure date is in a few short weeks. Boxes of food and equipment must be packed and mailed to post offices and towns near the trail where we'll take time out to resupply.

My family wonders if it is wise to leave now on a trip, but we have been planning it and waiting for the time to arrive for four years.

Before we began building, we hiked in the mountains nearly every summer for years. Todd and I found that we need to get away and spend some time with nature. It renews our spirits and enables us to work hard and persevere through immense projects—like building a log home. Going to the Sierra is not a luxurious vacation for us but a necessary pilgrimage.

When we do go up to our land to build, our pace is much more relaxed. This was supposed to be our big, full time building push. Now, even Todd is satisfied with whatever time we get to spend up there, so we're able to ease our pace.

We are finishing round eleven. Originally, we planned on twelve rounds of logs, but we recently took height measurements of the walls, and realized that the logs were so big that we had gained height quicker than we expected. There is plenty of headroom to allow you to easily walk under the tie logs. The work of putting the twelfth round, thirteen more logs, can be eliminated.

It's hard to believe that the walls of our house are now complete. Quite the milestone. It sounds like a big accomplishment but until the trusses and the roof are finished, our building will not be safe from rot. As Todd walks around the house, giving it one last check before departure, he discovers that one of the logs in the baby's room is very punky, like Styrofoam. Who knows how deeply it penetrates?

There is some rot on the floor joists, too. How much rot is too much? This is one of the biggest questions in our minds. We have patches of compromised wood here and there on the bottom few old logs, but nothing structurally dangerous at this point. We wonder though, how fast can it deteriorate? We wonder how much precipitation the logs can handle before there is severe damage. Once the roof is on, the rotting will be arrested.

We have a hard time believing the three months we'll be away will make that much difference; after all, the logs been exposed to the weather for three years. But there is that uncertain fear in our minds. Regardless, we're willing to take that chance because we really need a break from building.

A few days before our cross-country bus leaves for the coast, I visit my parents' house, for it will probably be sold by the time I return, and I'll never again be able to enter the house I grew up in. I have dreaded going back for weeks. Thinking of it brought a sick feeling to my insides, like when you walk into a hospital room to visit a loved one who is dying, and you haven't seen them in a while.

I don't recognize the red brick house when I pull up. Tears fill my eyes, making it difficult to see. The rusty glider and painted wooden rockers that I used to sit on in lazy summer afternoons and count cars going by when l was a kid are gone. The flowerpots with geraniums are gone. The canvas awnings are gone letting in sterile, bright light, illuminating the porch's nakedness. A carpet remnant bought as a runner to look good for perspective buyers lies tangled in the shrubs, blown off by a summer storm. Sheets of yellowed newspaper lie crumpled and stuck in the hedgerow. The metal "FOR SALE" sign swings and creaks on its hinge.

The house seems almost as important to me as my parents and saying goodbye feels almost as traumatic. It's what took place here—so many years of memories and sharing inside its walls and the yards surrounding it. It's hard to believe I can never come back.

Slipping my key into the big, oak door, I automatically look for the heavy drapes parting and my mother's smiling face peeking through the glass, turning the knob to let me in before I can turn my key. She always knew when I was coming home and hung around the living room to greet me. The drapes never move, and no face appears.

I push open the door and gasp. So cold! Like a tomb! Empty like my mother's dark Italian eyes when I saw her lying dead in her hospital bed. No sign of life anywhere. The smells are cold. Dampness. Mildew. A shut-in odor. They replace the smell of garlic and onions frying on the stove and the treats baking in the oven.

I close the door behind me and the sound echoes throughout the house, bouncing off the walls, no pictures or furniture to absorb the vibrations. Everything that could be picked up and moved is gone. There are signs that life took place here at one time. Indentations in the plush carpet tell where furniture once rested. Rectangles of bright paint show where pictures once hung. A gaping hole in the wall remains where the refrigerator once sat.

Most of our small yard was turned into a garden when Dad was alive. He put in twenty-eight tomato plants every year so he and Mom could jar quarts and quarts of her famous pasta sauce. These last years we mowed the weeds like grass and after this summer's rain, the garden looks like a jungle. In the basement, the pool table light hangs ridiculously low to the floor, with no balls or green felt table to illuminate.

The stillness inside is overwhelming. It's as though the house is lying in wait. In my old bedroom on the second floor, colorful paint blotches and rings of linseed oil stain the carpet. My palette had a tendency to dump, much to my parents' chagrin. Where my paintings once hung for viewing, nail holes cover the blue plaster walls like someone opened fire. I go into the bathroom and sit on the closed toilet. How many tearful hours I spent here as a teenager, late at night, arms folding tightly across my stomach, rocking back and forth and crying with menstrual cramps, the rusty radiator at my side that Mom used to make me scrub, never understanding why my younger brothers couldn't aim better.

I walk down the steps holding onto the wooden banister and think of the times I hung on those upper rungs as a child, crying to my parents to let me come down after I was sent to my room, punished for one thing or another, usually mouthing off. The same banister my hand glided over while the other held up my wedding gown while Dad waited at the bottom beaming. The same banister my skinny, weak father grabbed as he climbed to his bedroom, oxygen hose trailing behind, his fragile body fighting the losing battle of cancer, only a few years ago. My tears wet the wood on the banister as they fall.

I sit on the bottom step a long time, thinking about my past in this house and wondering about its future, about the family who will move in next. I realize, that despite its empty, abandoned look, this home is a living home, a symbol of warmth, security, comfort, and shelter from the outside world. What was here inside is not gone. The life and spirit that was once present lives in me, just like the love of my deceased parents. And I will transfer that love and spirit into my log home that we are building. Todd and I haven't been thinking about things like life and spirit happening inside our log walls. It seems more like a structure, a shell. We've made memories building it, but nothing compared to what will occur as we bring children into the world, raise them through their youth, and grow old within its strong log walls.

The feelings my parents' house has conjured up in me have given new meaning to our big question of why exactly we are building. Because we've put so much of ourselves into its creation, the memories we'll make inside will mean even more, not just to Todd and me, but to our children. Our log house is a gift, not only to the two of us, but also to our children and our children's children.

I rise and head toward the door, not feeling that I need to be here anymore. The Sierra calls me and then my log house and then the voices of my own unborn children. It is time to continue the flow. One generation has made room for the next.

14

The Trusses

WE ARE BACK FROM THE hike and boy have things changed. In the last three months our neighbors' homes have been finished and are occupied. Things have changed on our log house, too. The logs on the building have weathered gray and turned black from mildew. Fungus is growing in crusty, white strips between the logs. Mushrooms grow in the basement.

There is a pile of fifteen logs in the field a friend had offered to peel for us, so that we could have some peace of mind and leave as planned. Unfortunately, he ran into problems and the bark never got peeled. Had we done it ourselves in June, it would have only taken an afternoon. We did not realize how important this job would turn out to be. The logs are filled with more bore holes than I can count. We trashed other logs that had only a half dozen holes in them. These have hundreds and hundreds. We should have stayed home long enough to peel them. Perhaps we should have stayed home to also put on a roof. These thoughts are going through both of our minds.

Todd and I talk of fumigation. We know a couple who built a log kit that was infested with insects. They had a fumigation company put a huge plastic tent over their house and for $6,000 the deadly fumes killed every borer, carpenter ant, and boring bee in it. Todd says we could build another house for that amount of money. A little exaggerated but he's got a point. It actually looks like there's been structural damage to the logs. The trusses, which support the roof, must be built from the finest logs—the straightest, strongest, and most uniform. These insect-damaged logs had been earmarked for our trusses.

We also can't just order a few dozen more trees from our logger, for the trusses must be built out of seasoned wood, one to two years old. That's too long to wait. We must use these logs for our trusses. Fumigation, down the pike, sounds like a much better alternative. If we have it done before doors and windows are installed, the poison can get out of the house easier and our furniture, rugs, and counter tops would not be exposed to the fumes. What makes us feel so bad is it all could have been avoided by working one afternoon more.

When I peel bark off one of these logs, I find tiny slivers of wood mixed with round black specks, sticking to the log. The borers eat between the bark and the log before boring into the log itself. I slide an old wool sock over my hand and scrub the pulverized wood grounds off the log.

Trusses are big triangles of wood that support a roof.; in conventional building they are made of dimensional lumber; in our case, logs. Conventional buildings may have dozens of trusses spaced only sixteen inches apart and whacked together with 2x4s and nails. We only need to build five, but they will be monsters and must be mortised and tenoned together. This is precision carpentry and the most challenging of all the log work.

The truss design we have chosen is the king post truss, a truss well suited for supporting steep roofs and creating second-story living space. There are seven angles that must be fitted together at precisely forty-five and ninety degrees, *and* all five trusses must be exactly alike. As Todd shimmies one angle into position, other angles get moved out of place. Our log building teacher said they will drive you nuts and that's exactly what they are doing to Todd.

"What do the books say?" I ask.

"They say nothing," he says, but the truth is they say too much. Things like hypotenuses of right angles, the Pythagorean theorem, square roots . . .

"You read it and explain it to me." No way. Although Todd has always been good at math, my brain shuts down automatically when I try to ingest it. Todd decides to draw his forty-five- and ninety-degree angles and just wings it—takes his saw and makes a plunge cut for the mortises.

We've been feeling a bit overwhelmed lately. The day after we returned from California, we dove immediately into building and for six days, we never even bothered to unload our backpacks. Even our trail food bags are still in our packs with food in them! Todd has made a list of everything that needs to be done on the house: the roof, the greenhouse, the chimney, the foundation coating, the floors, the walls, windows, doors, plumbing, and wiring. I tell him to throw the list away and just think about the trusses now.

Things could be worse, for we now have a wonderful new friend who has been living with us and building full time: Steve Gomez from the coast of Massachusetts, another long-distance hiker and up until recently, an offshore fisherman. He sailed with the sailors in the *Perfect Storm* story but has since grown disillusioned with the industry. Some fishermen are scraping the eggs off the female lobsters to make a sale, and this unethical behavior is making it hard for Steve to continue in the trade, as much as he loves fishing in the open ocean. Steve has reached a turning point in his life. He's looking for a career change and thought he'd help us build while he considers alternatives.

THE TRUSSES

Steve's blue eyes sparkle beneath his worn blue baseball hat that's pulled down over his tight, auburn curls. I can see clear delineation of muscles in his thighs, even with thick denim jeans and long underwear on, and his forearms are very strong—a fringe benefit from hauling in nets laden with fish. Having another strong body around really helps on the building site.

Steve had originally planned to spend just the weekend, but his stay has already stretched to six days! We'd like to keep him for a month. Steve is even-tempered, extremely courteous, gracious, and kind. He doesn't talk a whole lot, which suits my quiet husband fine. He affectionately calls Todd "Old Dog" in his strong Massachusetts accent, and has the highest respect for him and what he is doing with his time and life. Having him help us on a daily basis gives me time to catch up on chores and my personal work.

We're giving our big blue tarps another chance. Chalk lines are snapped on the truss logs to flatten them and find angles. The string must be kept dry for the chalk to stick, so we stretch big ropes across

our septic area and hang a tarp like a huge tent over the area. "Under the Big Top," we call it. The tarp sags more and more as time goes by until it's lying on our heads when we work. It keeps those horrible chain saw fumes hanging low in our face. I stand on a nearby log and extend my arm to keep the plastic off Todd's back and head while he cuts. I turn my head and hold my breath. His saw is cranked into high gear as he flattens a log at full throttle, trigger completely depressed, buzzing like a swarm of bees.

When Todd cuts through a truss log, we can see the damage the borers have done more clearly. Some canals go six, eight inches deep, curving through the log. We sometimes find wormlike larvae, the color of the wood or pus, which is what their insides look like when you crush them. Their guts smell like turpentine, and why shouldn't they, considering their diet? Two dark brown "teeth" or jaws enable them to cut through solid wood. When they grind them, you can hear the sound a good distance away. They're going to sound lovely in our bedroom when we try to sleep. They are so much bigger than when they first went in, growing as they eat, and their canal grows in diameter to accommodate their bodies! How big will they get? They've grown from an eighth of an inch to the width of a pencil. Will they stop at an inch? Will their bodies grow to be two inches long? Will they come out in a few years and drop on my baby in her crib? Will my toddler pick them up and eat them? Our friend Frank says they may emerge as beetles. Equally horrible! Most larvae do, he says. They may come out to lay eggs and then their offspring may continue eating and boring, as well as their offspring, and their offspring! We must find out the length of their cycle! We are worried about the amount of damage these insects can do before the integrity of our logs is compromised.

Steve has returned to Massachusetts after a two-week stay. He wept when he left and said, "I can't believe I'm really going." While he was here, we got three of our five trusses built. Living together went remarkably well. There was never any friction, tension, or feelings of lost privacy. And he slept right on our living room floor. The only time Todd and I were alone was in our own bed. I missed Todd's show of

affection on the building site, for he is more reserved when someone else is around, but by the end of Steve's second week, even that had changed, and he'd begun to show his true nature. We are so much further ahead in our work because of Steve's help. But the real gift is the wonderful friendship that evolved while he lived with us and worked by our sides.

It's early November and the autumn rains have arrived. We sit in the truck cab to have lunch for it is the warmest, driest place. From the warmth of the cab, we're trying to figure how our second-floor joists will be laid. Todd would like to have leftover logs cut into lath for our slate roof, but he needs to figure which logs will be needed for the joists before he can take the remainder to the sawmill. Todd cannot force himself to figure out future steps that are beyond his present knowledge. If I push him, he gets that crazed look in his eyes and tells me, "I feel like I'm getting a brain tumor."

That kind of talk really upsets me. I believe that your body and mind are most definitely connected, and if you pump enough negative thoughts into it, your body will oblige, but you can't be involved in a prolonged project like this and not get fatigued and discouraged. We just have to have faith that when we arrive at those future steps in the building process, we will have acquired the knowledge we need to work out the problems.

Todd has all the time in the world to think and figure now. He has suddenly injured himself. He's lying flat on his back, immobile. I have to help him go to the bathroom. I have to feed him, for he cannot even raise his arm to bring a fork to his lips. When I go out to work one night, I set him up on the sofa with a drink of water and his woodworking books, the phone, and a lamp. I cover him with blankets and fill the woodstove to the brim to keep him warm. I neglect to leave enough airspace in the firebox to burn the wood, however, for I pack it so full. He is startled from a nap by the room filling with smoke, causing him to forget his injury and jump off the sofa!

With the help of a rigid clipboard to write on, he shares his feelings:

"All five trusses were cut and fit and ready for step two—raising them onto the building. Cindy and I went up to take down the tarps that sheltered the trusses. Sometime between pulling down the tarp and folding it, and untying its support rope on the tree, I must have made an abnormal twist that injured my back. Bending and twisting became harder to do with each passing minute, until I was incapable of doing anything but lie completely flat to prevent unbearable pain from shooting up my back and spazzing my muscles.

"I'm not really bummed about not building. I'm just not happy with my position. While lying here, I began to think of how fortunate we've been with our lack of injuries and accidents. Perhaps this is just a painful reminder to exercise caution and safety in the truss raising ahead."

Four days later, Todd has a miraculous recovery. John Vincent from Massachusetts is coming back to help, and Todd wants to work . . . the power of the mind over matter.

This morning Todd rolls over in bed and hugs me, saying, "I feel like it's Christmas, honey."

"Why?"

"Because today is the day we raise our first truss!" He is very excited. Not only is John Vincent here, but Steve Gomez has also returned. It takes hours to get the rigging right before we can actually pull up the truss. There's never a lot for me to do when men are helping us. If Todd says he needs something, they bolt to get it, beating me to it. I stand around and get colder and colder. Todd's so intent on making sure that our guests have jobs to keep them occupied, that he forgets to periodically give me jobs.

Things have changed on the building site. I'm not the right-hand helper anymore. Since Todd quit his job, I have been supporting us financially. I'm away from the building site more than before, and these helpers free me up to do that. I am grateful. And for the most part I have accepted this new situation, but there are some things I can't seem to let go of.

Because these men are stronger and are used to working with Todd when I'm not around, they simply bypass me and don't include me in the work process when I *am* there. I'm happy to give up some of the difficult work but not all of the work. I still need to feel that it's my house and that I'm building it. Sometimes I ask Todd what he plans on doing for the next step, but he occasionally gets upset with my questioning. I need to understand what is going on and feel a part of it. It's good for Todd to be in charge, delegate authority, and work with other men on his own. He used to say he couldn't work with others, but I think that is no longer true. These men feel proud and good about the fact that they are learning new skills. They respect Todd and want his respect and want to know at least some of what he knows. Todd's subconscious knows this and the positive reinforcement encourages him to continue teaching, leading, and sharing. I know what is going on, too. It's just sometimes difficult for me to take a back seat or no seat at all. I, in turn, must learn to step back, even though that is the opposite of my personality.

By early afternoon, we are finally ready to raise the truss. We built the trusses on the ground but break it down into four pieces of log, which we pull up to the building individually with the skyline rope. Then, while standing on a makeshift platform of planks high on the building, the truss is reassembled. It is bolted back together and placed in position to be raised by the skyline with the steadying help of men on ropes. I stand on the planks with my camera by the truss and get ready to record this moment in history. The day is raw and cold. I pull my purple wool balaclava over my face and let down my hair to warm my neck.

As the truck starts to pull the top of the truss, the bottom slides backward, out of position. "HOLD IT!" Todd yells. Time out to lever and come-along the truss back into position and build braces against the wall so the bottom cannot kick out. "Let's try it again!"

The wood creaks and moans as the truss point pivots skyward, until it's standing straight up and down, perpendicular to the building. While the skyline supports it from above, two men steady it on either side by pulling on the ropes attached to it and make minor adjustments to its position. Todd, meanwhile, climbs onto the truss, with a level in hand. "Pull it to my left a tad!" he yells from his perch. The big truss creaks and moves with Todd's feet dangling from the collar tie high in the air. When it's level, they nail boards to the skyline tree and brace it so it cannot move.

When the excitement is over, I go over to the "living room" and sit in the space where our brown, hand-me-down easy chair will go and look up at the truss. I just can't get over how high it is—twenty-four feet! I imagine our six-foot, stained-glass window that will be placed inside the triangle, letting in morning light. I imagine the balcony and the cathedral ceiling above. It's really turning into a house, and a grand house at that. Actually, it looks more like a church with just the raising of this one truss.

Fortunately for us, Steve decides to stay and help for another two weeks. After a week of working on the trusses together, I learn something very interesting from him. He has grown extremely frustrated about not doing enough work and not knowing enough skills. He'd like to be taught more; he'd like to learn everything. Truss work is precise work. Todd can't afford the time to train Steve in chainsawing or take the chance that he could do irreplaceable damage.

Yesterday, for a change, I did a job at the site that I know how to do well, leaving Steve below on the ground, asking if there was something he could do. There wasn't, not at that particular time. The tables were turned.

As the day grew late, he became increasingly disgusted with himself and had problems nailing bowed lumber. He cursed and swore every few seconds, which is very uncharacteristic of him. Finally, he declared, "Why would any chick want to get interested in me? I can't do anything. I spent too damn much time fishing!"

"Now hold on there, Steve. Where's all this coming from?" I ask.

"No one wants a husband who spends two months at a time at sea. I can't go back to fishing. I need to find different work."

Here he was hoping to find a new occupation while staying with us. Perhaps log house construction? Perhaps woodworking? Perhaps art? None of these skills can be learned in a few weeks. His time with us is drawing to a close, and he doesn't have any more answers of what to do with his life than when he arrived.

I explain why we decided to refrain from teaching chainsawing to our helpers and why there is a limit to what Todd will allow him, or anyone, to do on the building.

"We get very possessive with this house. People might come and help us like yourself and Mick and John and put in a lot of hours, but it can never compare to our four years of constant work. There is also the mental anguish we have gone through, of not knowing what to do and how to do it. The hours we've spent in bed at night with Todd all perplexed and me trying to calm his fears and doubts.

"Yeah, it would be nice to come and build and go home and never have to figure anything out," Todd adds.

"Todd has a lot more responsibility than I do, as far as learning new jobs and making progress. I do a lot of other jobs but one of my most important is keeping him calm and happy and emotionally stable. That can be a really big job, just as big as chainsawing."

After I finish explaining, Steve quickly says, "Well, I'm here to do anything you want me to do. I want you to know I will try anything new, but it's up to you. This is your baby."

"Thanks Steve. It does feel much like our child." I immediately feel closer to him. It has gotten a little more difficult living together, because of the duration of time and the close quarters, but it has nothing to do with Steve. He is marvelous. My own frustrations feel easier to accept and deal with when I know that someone like Steve has frustrations of his own, too. He feels like my brother, and Todd and I feel nothing but the utmost respect and love for him.

Today is purlin day. These logs will support the rafters and will be placed halfway down the sides of the five trusses and run the length of the building. Since the rafters cannot stretch from the top of the roof to the eaves without support, the middle of each rafter will rest on these purlins. We raise a purlin on the skyline rope and get ready to pull it down the cable to the far end of the building and the three trusses. It's now much more difficult to move suspended logs since there are three trusses directly beneath the skyline and in the way. While someone pulls the skyline rope to move the log, someone else must pull the log out and away from the standing trusses. Steve and I are on ropes, under the suspended log. Todd is up on the building getting ready to guide it in place.

"*This is really dangerous!*" Todd yells, as Steve and I try to maneuver the log. "*If this log breaks loose and slams me, I'm going to be a hurting pup!*"

He continually repeats the same words over and over, screaming all the time, while the purlin swings and bangs into the trusses. I suddenly realize that I am the only one who has a clear view of what is going on, so I start barking orders.

"*Steve, pull down! Now pull up!*" After we finally get it in place, Todd is still yelling instead of talking in a moderate tone and so am I. It takes a long time to calm our beating hearts down.

A few days later, truss #4 goes up smoothly enough with the help of Todd's brother, Brendt, since Steve has returned to his home in Massachusetts. We request helpers to help raise these beasts. It would be impossible without them.

Truss #5, however, is a different story. All of the previous trusses were put together lying flat on the building, so when they were raised, they pivoted right on their final resting place. We cannot do that with this last truss, for it would extend fifteen feet *beyond* the building into the air. Even if there were something to assemble it on, it would still be impossible, for the oak skyline tree is in the way. With the help of my brother Dave and brother-in-law John, we instead build the truss ten feet back on the building from where it will ultimately rest. When we begin to raise it, we must not only lift it up, but must also slide the bottom out to the end of the building.

Everything goes according to plan and all five trusses are up on the building. The next day, Mick comes and helps us put the last purlins and half of the ridgepole up. Getting this important log into the air is a tricky job. Since the peak of our roof is actually higher than the cable, the skyline can only lift the ridgepole log so far and then it is up to human strength to get it higher. Getting the ridgepole onto the trusses is also very tricky. Before the trusses were raised, Todd had drilled a hole in the very top of each one, where a metal rod was pounded into and left to extend six inches. The ridgepole has corresponding drilled holes that will fit over the one-inch rebar pins that protrude from the top of each truss. Once the ridgepole is locked in place, they will prevent the ridgepole from moving. It's not as easy as it sounds. With the help of some shaky ramps made of planks, Mick and Todd manage to push and slide the ridgepole log up to the pins. They are fearful, however, that the log will roll over to the other side and fall to the ground before they can get it centered over the pin. With the men's combined strength, they lift each end of the log up and onto the three pins. It is nerve-racking work and both physically and mentally draining, but they are successful.

The next day, Todd and I are all alone to put the other half of the ridgepole up—the very final log that will be placed on the building.

Each morning this week, I found him lying wide awake and motionless in bed. He's been figuring out mechanics and procedures for lifting trusses, purlins, and ridgepoles. He's been imagining rigging setups, planning jobs for people, and going through each process step-by-step in his mind to find the most efficient way of doing things.

"I've got the whole thing figured out, honey. I know how we're going to raise the ridgepole and I can't foresee any major problems."

"How do you figure these things out?" I ask. "How do these ideas come?"

"It seems like there's a way to do everything. Nothing, so far, has been impossible. I know what I have to work with: my slings, the skyline, the come-along, etc. I know how far to swing things. I know how far I can push things. I know what worked before and what failed. I can mostly predict how things will react. It's just the unexpected, the unpredictable, that I didn't plan for that I must be ready to deal with.

"We learned so much from this building. What we can move with a plank as a lever is amazing. And if you learn balance points on logs, you can do so much with very little strength. Things like gaining length on a log by rolling it backward and putting it on an angle. Things you can't find in a book, but small bits of knowledge that made this all possible."

Fortunately, we only find a few kinks in the whole procedure. Todd had expected the skyline pulley to get the log higher than it does. He also didn't expect the cable to sag as much as it does, but we come-along it up the remaining inches to get it onto the plank. We slide the log up the plank together and onto a chunk of wood that he has placed next to each of the two truss pins, a little higher than the metal rod. While Todd guides the ridgepole over the pin, I take the heavy hammer and knock each chunk of wood into the air, and the ridgepole falls into place.

I climb down from the twenty-four-foot height, take a bow saw, and cut down a white pine sapling near the house—the same kind of wood that our house is made from. I carry it up to Todd and hand it to him. He climbs out onto the ridgepole and nails the tree straight up against the cut end of the ridgepole. His dark green insulated suit and the dark green bough silhouette against the brilliant blue sky overhead. It's a Scandinavian tradition that after the frame of the roof is raised, a piece of the forest is nailed to the roof to pay homage to the trees and keep the evil spirits forever above and away from the new home. As author Tracy Kidder says in his book *House*, "Having taken wood from the tree, builders bring the tree back to the wood, the tree becomes the house, and in ceremony, the house becomes the tree."

When Todd hands the hammer back to me I see that he is crying. By the time we are down on the ground and look up at the house, he is sobbing hard. I hold him in my arms and we cry together.

"It's done," he says. "The log work is done. We really, really did it. Yesterday we had a major obstacle to overcome; today, there are no more. No more logs to peel. No more logs to put up. I feel so lucky. So proud to have done it. All the things that could have gone wrong and didn't. I just feel so grateful." We cling to each other, hold each other's hands tightly and say a prayer, thanking God for always being by our side through it all.

"It's been really intense lately," Todd admits, as we load tools in the truck. "I've had so much anxiety, trying to figure things out. It's different doing stuff that's a little shady. When I'm up on top of the building, I could drop a log and wreck a lot of things, including my own body. It was such an adrenaline rush to be up there. No matter how many safety precautions I took, I never knew if it was going to work the way I expected. There isn't a lot of room for error. I had to watch our helpers, be aware of where they were, what they were doing, if they were doing it right. I hadn't realized how much it had been building up inside of me until now.

"There's so much more to this than just moving logs. The laws of physics have been essential, and I'll probably continue using them throughout my life. But it's the fact that we kept going. We stuck it out and persevered. We started out with a dream and now we have a log house and that means more than anything."

HINTS & TIPS:

- The end result of the integrity of your logs will depend on when they were cut, what time of the year, and how quickly you work them. By autumn, at least in our area of the US, insects will finish up eating the cambium layer between the bark and the solid wood and begin to burrow in for the winter. It is best to peel the bark off at this point, to prevent internal insect damage, and it is easier, since the insects loosened the bark. This will vary however, from state to state and climate to climate.
- If your building is small, you will not have to deal with trusses as they are only necessary for large spans. You could do a shed roof design or another, to simplify. Our log home has a steep roof to create living space on the second floor. If you incorporate log knee walls, you will have to do quite a bit more of logwork, too.
- Gratitude is a virtue that will always serve you well in life and that includes doing a very hard and dangerous task like building

a log home. Exercise it always and acknowledge and celebrate milestones and accomplishments on a regular basis. Adopting this attitude toward the act of building will help you go on to create a whole life of gratitude.

THE FIFTH YEAR
1989

15

Separation

THE LOG WORK IS COMPLETE, and we have reached a momentous milestone in our house construction, but there are many more jobs to be done. Todd is putting up the rafters all by himself. He is splicing one hundred fifteen-foot boards of poplar into fifty thirty-foot-long rafters. He says he can't use me now. The rafters are too big and heavy for me to handle. And I won't crawl out onto the ridgepole and purlins. Todd doesn't mind heights; I get dizzy and light-headed. The rafters are even hard for Todd to handle. He first leans each fifteen-foot rafter against the building. Then he climbs up and pulls the rafter until its bottom edge is resting on the top of the wall. Then he moves up to the purlin and pulls the rafter until its bottom end is resting on a nail in the purlin that he placed there to hold it until he can nail it. Then, he goes up to the ridgepole to begin bolting them and nailing them together. He must get up and down off the building with every plank he puts up, at least a hundred times in a day. The boards are all twisted and warped. He really has to slam those long, fat, forty-penny nails to get them into the seasoned wood. My strong brother David was helping for a while and *he* kept bending the nails.

I don't know how Todd does it. I don't know how he lifts those planks and maneuvers them up so high all by himself. I don't know how his one hand can hold the heavy two-by-eight-inch board still, keep it in place, while the other hand nails.

While Todd toils on the building, I stay home and write. Magazine articles consume my life. My head swims with ideas for new pieces and ones already contracted. The creative juices are flowing like a river, and I can't shut them off. Since I've been the sole breadwinner, I feel obligated to give it my all. And Todd is taking his new job to heart. His head is consumed with plans, figures, designs, and procedures. He wakes up in the morning and I see it in his eyes. He's thinking about "the roof."

When Todd is done with the rafters, we once again get our big blue tarps out and try to cover the building. The twenty-five rafters on each side should be enough skeletal support to prevent wind from getting underneath like before and acting like a sail.

Todd climbs like a monkey. He walks straight up the forty-five-degree-angle truss in his rubber-soled Sorrel boots, with each hand on a rafter to balance. You'd think he had suction cups on his boots, the way he motors up so quickly and confidently. I remain on the ground, head bent back so far it hurts because he's up so high, and I repeat, "Please be careful."

He shinnies across the ridgepole, pulling the open tarps down the building. Besides being very scary at twenty-five feet in the air, it is an extremely painful job, for the ridgepole now has two boards nailed to it at right angles to accept slate. The wooden point digs into his crotch. He's not a happy builder. I run from one side of the building to the other, freeing the tarp and guiding it around rafter edges. We take our ropes and lace them through the grommets and tie the big blue roof down. Finally, after two and a half years, our building is covered and safe from rain.

Two days of heavy rains pass. We are thrilled that all this mildew and fungus-causing precipitation isn't touching our logs. When we return to the land, however, we find the tarps filling with wind and flapping off the building. They rise into the air and then fall like the giant lungs of a monster. The metal grommets have pulled loose. At the two dormer holes that Todd left without rafters, the tarp sags and collects water until hundreds of gallons are hanging through the openings. Todd climbs onto the roof and tries to pull up on the tarp full of water. I run to get our pike pole, a tool used for pushing trees over when they're being cut, and at the same time, push up on the tarp from below. In my excited haste, I forget that the pole has a metal point on it and puncture the plastic, letting all the water spill onto the floor and the rotting floor joists anyway. "Hurry and get buckets!" he commands. I catch what I can.

Four days later, trying to catch water in buckets seems ridiculous. It's been raining and snowing ever since. We stay mostly indoors now. My husband is at home with me in the same little room all day long. The upstairs is too cold to work, plus I'd have to drag the kerosene heater up and down the narrow wooden steps every day. Todd looks through cookbooks, lies around on the sofa, takes a jar out to the recycling bin, makes a trip to the outhouse, picks up the mail, and keeps me from my work. Since he's in the same room, I almost have to ignore him to get anything done. My concentration breaks, and I look up from my papers. The refrigerator is making funny noises. It sounds like it's straining. It acts this way every winter when it's cold in the house. The light doesn't always come on when you open the door and I wonder then, if it's not dead, or dying.

"I'm not crazy about spending another winter in this house," he interrupts me, as he stands by the wood cookstove, hot cocoa in hand, rubbing his bottom against the warm, shiny chrome. When I finish my thought, I put down my pen.

"Frank thinks we should forget the tarps and put the roof on," he continues.

"In January?" I ask. "In the middle of winter? That job was supposed to wait for mild spring. Climbing around an icy, steep roof sounds very dangerous." This is his first winter at home full time.

"Let's do it and get it done," Todd says. "I want to spend next winter in a warm house."

And so, donned in forest green, insulated, subzero suits, we go up to the land with our roofing gear. Ten degrees—a good temperature for starting. I bought Todd's insulated one-piece suit for him for Christmas, and mine was given to me by my girlfriend whose husband left her and this suit behind. It's a little long, as he is six-foot-three, but it does the job. Todd finally decides which logs he wants for the second floor and takes the remaining pieces to the sawmill to be cut into roofing lath. The one-by-two-inch strips are riddled with borer holes. If they chewed on an angle across the wood, the holes came out very oblong in shape. I test each piece for strength by pushing on it between two sawhorses and they invariably snap at the greatest concentration of holes. Those get tossed in favor of lath with more structural integrity. I cut the strips to order, because our rafters are bowed, the intervals don't fall at exactly two-foot sections. I hand up lath, more copper nails, his can of tar, and a putty knife, for some of our recycled slates have too many holes in them.

The roof we're putting on is mostly recycled slate. A few years back, Demolition King Uncle Iggie was taking down a large brick building at the Wernersville State Mental Hospital. Because the building was no longer being used, the state ordered its removal. The building was covered with twenty-year-old slate, and since slate is said to last at least fifty to seventy-five years, we decided that slate would be our roof choice. Frank and Lila, along with a few other friends, dedicated a three-day weekend as we climbed up on the vacant building and carefully removed the slate off the roof. With Frank's knowledge of slate work, which he gleaned from helping his builder father, he was able to instruct us all in the tedious job. He taught us how to ring slate with the slate hammer and listen for cracks as well as identify soft slate—inferior slates that we wouldn't want on our house. We gathered all the copper nails we removed and gave them to Todd's grandfather who made a little jig so he could hammer them straight which would allow us to reuse them. We salvaged over thirty-two pounds of nails that would have cost four dollars a pound—a big savings. We worked feverishly those three days, for the following Monday the building was scheduled for demolition.

Had we not altered the original truss design we would have had more than enough slate. Unfortunately, the steeper trusses made the roof surface much larger. Together with the roof's four- and six-foot overhangs needed to protect the logs, we need three thousand twelve-by-twenty-four-inch slates. We only had enough recycled slate for two thirds of the roof and had to purchase one third new for $2,400, about the same cost as a conventional twenty-year roof (back in the 1980s). We figure we'd still be ahead with the recycled slate since it will last as many years as two conventional roofs.

Slating the roof goes more smoothly than expected. Only at the end of a row is the flow interrupted when a specially sized slate needs

to be cut. Over by our stacked piles of slate, we have a large, sawed-off stump that the point of the T-shaped slate anvil is inserted into. With a nail and a ruler, I scratch the desired width onto the gray stone. I lay that line right along the edge of the narrow anvil and chop away with the neck of my slate hammer which doubles as a cutting edge. The broken, unwanted pieces fall to the ground by my right side. Then I take my hammer point and tap two holes in the slate on the underneath side for the hole breaks out clean there. On the other side, the stone breaks out into a tiny flared hole, which is perfect for the seated nail head. If the head couldn't be recessed, it would sit above the flat surface and cause the slates that lay on top of them to break when they are hammered against it. I have to apply the perfect amount of force—too much will make the hole too big; too small and I have to hit it again at the exact same spot only slightly harder. It takes skill.

After six rows of straight slate are laid, I begin to scallop them, for decorative purposes. Scalloped slates are just rectangles with the corners cut off at a forty-five-degree angle. Todd cuts a pattern out of a piece of old wall paneling so I can lay it on my slate as a guide and draw my angles.

After we slate six more rows, we reach the dormer holes and slating comes to a halt. We used to spend many evening hours sitting side by side on the couch examining our log home picture books. We'd look for photographs of specific things like railing designs, porches, or chimneys that we might want in our own home. During one of these sofa sessions, Todd said, "Let's build dormers. They will bring light and more space to the second-floor rooms." No books we owned contain any information on how to build them, however, and the local university library gives no clues, either. All we have is a skeletal drawing on one of the covers of our wood framing books.

With that book in hand, Todd climbs up on the roof and tries to copy what he sees. His furniture-making skills are really coming in handy: framing with lumber, cutting angles, making joints. "If you understand the principles of level, square, and plumb," he tells me, "you can build anything."

"Sure hope I have enough scrap lumber to build these dormers," he says. "Half my nails are too short; the other half are too long. What I need are medium nails, but we wouldn't want to buy any. Don't want to spend any money on these dormers. Gotta do them for free."

I shake my head in disbelief at his German frugality, but the house is really happening. We've salvaged lumber, salvaged slate, salvaged windows. When he gets to the dormer flashing, he becomes completely stumped. At the point where the peak of the dormer roof meets the roof of the house, there is a hole the size of a pencil where the flashing intersects. He doesn't have a metal crimper to form a special piece and he doesn't own a soldering gun to close up the hole. If he doesn't do something, it will leak. He gets himself worked up and says, "I'm going to rip the whole thing off!"

"Wait a minute. This problem must be encountered every time a dormer is built. There has to be a solution."

"Yeah. Rip the whole thing off," he repeats.

"Oh, cool off!" I tell him.

"Why don't you go home," he tells me. "You drove separately."

I pack up and leave. There's been nothing for me to do since he began work on the flashing. I've been sitting around and reading the paper, my head immersed in the magazine articles that I'm writing.

Back at home, Frank calls and I unload.

"Your heads are in separate places," he says. "You're trying to make a living. He's trying to finish the house."

"We're on new jobs all the time, Frank. Jobs that Todd isn't sure of the procedure. He says to me, 'This is what we are going to do today, and I could use you here,' and I say, 'Okay, I'll come.' And I go along, and he hits a snag, or it takes much longer than he anticipates or he

isn't sure what to do, and there I stand, frustrated, with lots of things on my mind and building isn't one of them.

"He's so hard on himself, too," I continue. "He thinks he should know how to do every job or be able to figure it out all by himself simply because he is a man. Where does he get this from?"

Before I hang up, Lila grabs the phone and says to me laughing, "If you can get through with this house building and still be friends, it may be your biggest accomplishment."

While Todd and I prepare dinner that night, we both excuse ourselves as we pass in the small kitchen but say little else. We move each other's ingredients that are getting in the way of our own creations to the side. After we eat, I try to help him understand my frustration. He keeps repeating, though, through my whole talk, "You don't like to work at the land. You don't want to come."

"That's not true," I say. "I just have other things pulling me besides the house—my writing."

"The only thing on my mind is the house. When I can't use your help, there are lots of other jobs you can do."

"Like what?"

"Like figure out room sizes and then how much flooring we need. Figure out how many two-by-fours we need to frame out the interior walls. Stud out the walls. Notch the floor joists and flatten them. It all depends on what your capabilities are, what you're willing to learn."

"Would you really take my word for all those figures? Wouldn't you figure it out for yourself anyway? Would you really prefer *me* to do those jobs?"

"The way I see it," he says, "You have three choices. One, sit and write and help me when you can, and be frustrated in between. Two, stay home. And three, learn new jobs."

"There's a limit to what I can fit into my head, creatively and energy wise. And there's a limit to what I can do time-wise, too. I have to write. I have to support us."

I sometimes feel like I want to be part of every single step of the building. I want to share in it so I can understand each step. I feel bad when I miss out on an important step like the rafters. I also want to make it easier for Todd. Yet I still need space and time to do my own work. There's a difference in our priorities now.

I know in our life ahead, there will be times when as a couple, we will lean on one of us more than the other for financial security. (In the course of just building this home, Todd was the primary breadwinner at one time and now I am.) Our interest levels may not be the same, either. As individuals, we each have passion for different things. (Todd is not involved in my writing, and usually that is okay.) As a couple, we must learn how to gift each other the individual time that they personally need, be there to help the other as much as we can, not expect more from the other than they can deliver.

During some periods in life, one of us may also be doing more of the jobs needed to run a home and a family. Todd might now be more responsible for building our home, but, in the future, I might be more responsible for the daily task of raising and educating our children, because that particular job might be easier or well-suited. Jobs shift over the course of a lifetime, but in a healthy relationship, it seems to even out. Relationships and roles must be allowed to remain fluid, flexible in order to survive and flourish. They ebb and flow, just like our strengths and weaknesses. When one of us is having a particularly hard time in life, through dealing with emotional trauma or physical injury, for example, the other must step up, do more than their share at that time, not resent, knowing life will even out over time.

After we run out of our holey pine lath, Todd must go to the sawmill and buy more. He chooses a sawmill that claims to have pine, which is hard to find. The sawyer says to Todd, "I have some poplar. That should work, too." Although Todd does not want poplar, because it is a considerably harder wood than pine, he says nothing. And now I know why he didn't want it.

The lath is green and the saw feels like it sticks or gums up when I cut the strips to length. The metal saw twangs and vibrates back and forth as I try to cut. It will not take a nail, for the wood is too hard and cracks. I must drill every hole for Todd before I send the pieces up. We have no power yet, so we borrow our neighbor's cordless drill. It works for fifteen minutes, in which time I break his two drill bits.

Now we have to wait until tomorrow and get our own drill bits. In the meantime, Todd decides to put the living room skylight in. Together we figure where the center of the room will be. While I write in my journal in the truck, Todd puts in the framework. "Let's check it out," I say when the job is complete. We walk over to the spot and I immediately say, "It's in the wrong place."

"Oh shit!" he says. As he yanks the boards out with his Wonder Bar, he ruins both boards and has to cut two more two-by-eights by hand since both chain saws are too dull to use.

The next day is no better. I'm using our hand drill today fitting a round bit into a triangular-shaped chuck. When I pull the drill out, the bit often stays in the wood. I don't seem to have enough strength to make the chuck so tight that the bit won't slip out, nor do I have enough strength to loosen it once it comes out to put it back in. My arms ache from drilling and sawing. I'm just not that strong. I am so frustrated that I start to cry.

"You can go home," Todd says. This isn't what I want to hear. I want to work. I want to help. I don't want to have to work so hard just so that I can get strong to do all these things. My hands get so fatigued from sawing lumber and cutting slate. They feel like they have growing pains. Todd's hands have increased enormously since we began this project. If it keeps up at this rate, he'll have paws instead of hands. I'm so tired of this house.

Our hiking friend Dave Walp just got laid off from his construction job and wants to help us get our roof up. Dave reminds me of a Norseman with his full red beard. He looks like he ought to have a gold pointed helmet pressing down on his red eyebrows. He is short and his little belly reminds me of a hobbit. He is good-natured and loves conversation. For lunch, he often stops at a farmer's market for fried mushrooms, or a deli for baked beans, or a bakery for jam-filled soft cookies as he makes his daily hour-long drive to our land. There's often leftover food from his lunch and he always throws it in our lunch box, so we can eat it as an evening snack. He's not possessive with his tools, either, and generously leaves them with Todd so he can continue using them during the week. Todd and I are touched by his long commute and the money he spends on gas to get to our place, on top of his hard work and time spent building.

I am overjoyed that Todd has a helper, and I take the day off from cutting lath to stoke the home fires and write. I need a break. During the course of the afternoon, our full half-gallon glass jar of honey slides off the top of the wood cookstove's warming oven and breaks all over the top of the range, which is cranked high with heat. The honey bubbles and smokes and fills the house with the smell of burning sugar. It pours over the side and onto the loose bricks laid on the linoleum floor around the stove legs. I take each brick outside to a bucket of hand-pumped water and scrape them with a wire brush. I mop up the honey on the floor, now mixed with dust balls and wood fragments that have fallen through the bricks over the years. Underneath the burner plates, there are black, hardened bubbles of burnt honey, looking like lava flow. In black, greasy water, I scour the stove parts with steel wool. The whole job takes hours and Todd returns home to find little more than a few sentences written.

He reports, "Dave said that this is an awful lot of work for one or two people, especially without power. It doesn't feel like a labor of love, to me. It feels more like a death sentence."

This weekend we are slating around the skylights. Todd asks me to cut a lot of "special orders"—L-shaped slates to fit around the corners. I stay down below and cut them, for I have gotten good at it. In between, I sit on the dirt hill watching Todd and Dave work. Mick is here, too, since it's Sunday. There is even less for him to do so he feeds the campfire with the scrap pieces from the lath, making the blaze so high and hot you can hardly get near it when we take a break.

With all this company, you'd think Todd would be having a good day, but this poplar lath is giving him the worst time yet. He bangs his hammer and swears and bangs some more and swears some more and yells, "Cut me another slate! I broke this one, too!"

Dave pokes up his head and his torso between two layers of lath. He hands Todd slates as he needs them. He is talking to Todd the whole time he is swearing, chattering about why the slates are probably breaking. Todd doesn't answer. He knows why they're breaking. Dave is only trying to calm him down. I laugh to myself as I watch them. Todd walks back and forth across the roof in disgusted haste, almost stepping on Dave's head or shoving his rear end in his face as he works on the lath. It's hard for Dave to duck down in time, like a prairie dog, for he can only fit through the hole in one direction.

Since he's been roofing, Todd has gotten quite a gutter mouth. At home tonight, he unloads: "I have to nail so fuckin' hard to get those nails into that lath. I have to concentrate so fuckin' hard on my aim to hit the nail head and not the slate. Then I look over and see that the slate beside it got jarred loose from the banging. I keep looking ahead for a rafter and then I get excited when one draws close for I know that that particular nail will hit something solid. On the lath, the nail heads bend over and I can't pull them out so all I can do is bang them flat.

"The slates are cracked. Some are hanging on by one nail. You'd think I was roofing a chicken house. I'm already trying to figure what kind of roof I'm going to put on *next*. All because that dumb shit at the sawmill gave me that poplar. 'Oh, it won't give you any problem,' he said. I could wring his neck!" It all makes me laugh, for had he been more assertive at the sawmill, he wouldn't be in this pickle.

Roofing must stop for a while, until the chimney is built. We'll slate our roof all the way up to the top and then run our overlapping ridgeline slates out as the very last step. We must wait for warmer weather, however, before we can mix mud to build the chimney. In the meantime, Todd decides to tackle framing in the gable ends of the house. As expected, they present a major problem. How do you close the gap between the round truss log and the slate roof? Todd planned poorly and didn't put a rafter right above the log so he could nail onto it. What is directly above the outside trusses is slate, which can't be nailed to. He is distraught. When we come home from building it is late and already growing dark. Fog hugs the mountaintop, and I ask if the truck lights are on. "Yes, they're on!" Todd snaps. I say nothing. He's always losing his patience and often snapping at me. When I try to find out what is going on, he has no words.

I've never seen my husband so depressed for such a long time. Building is really taking its toll on him. He thought it would be exciting and fun to get into these different jobs, but what he's discovering is that there are many more things he doesn't know how to do. Every new job is no longer a fun challenge, but something to knock him down. He also has so many jobs, he doesn't know which one to work on. Should he begin the chimney so he can close up the roof? Although it's March, it's too cold for the mortar to set for it still drops below freezing at night. He could frame out the gable ends, but he really could use power for that. But before the electric ditch can be dug, the foundation needs to be stuccoed so the excavator can backfill while he's here. He has so many decisions to make that his mind feels overwhelmed. He does nothing instead. He lies around in the evenings with this incredibly sullen look on his face and usually allows his entire evening to pass without accomplishing anything.

I'm normally a happy, positive person, but Todd is driving me crazy. I didn't cry this much since my parents died and I think I handled that better. I told Todd I'd call him from work today and see what frame of mind he is in and decide then whether to stay at the library or come home. That upset him. He looked like he was going to cry. He said everything is going wrong in his life, and now his wife doesn't want to be around him.

I try to work through his depression for him by discussing and analyzing. Actually, I talk and he listens. I ask him questions, but they only send him deeper inward. It used to work. I said if he wanted me to help him with his problems, then I am going to have to go back to school for a psychology degree, because I have exhausted my knowledge. I've used up all my strategies. In the morning, he lies around with his head buried between our two pillows as though he were hiding. He mopes around and I can't get any work done and there are writing deadlines I must meet. This morning I make him repeat over and over with the thumbs-up sign: "I'm going to have a really good day today." He thought "really" was a little too much to ask.

Last night he tried to make homemade butter in the electric mixer but only got one pound from three quarts of cream, instead of the two pounds he was supposed to get. The mixer sprayed cream all over the counter, our shelves, and the walls. He sat down, defeated. He couldn't even deal with cleaning it up. "Tomorrow," he said, "'I don't plan on building. I feel like quitting over there and going out to get a job."

"That isn't what we need. We need a house," I say.

"Why can't we stay here?" he asks. "There's nothing wrong with this place. I'm starting to like it more," he says, as the wind rattles the panes.

This will probably pass. I get scared, though, thinking how much worse it could get, or how long it could go on. Lila wonders if this house-building endeavor isn't too much for him. I can hear in my head what our log building teacher often repeated—how difficult it is for couples to stay together throughout these projects. I can see how it could happen if there isn't a lot of love. The worst is behind us—the logwork—or so we both assumed until we arrived at this point. It's been three years since we started on the house, and we have less than a year to go. You'd *think* the worst would be over. I wonder if we'd do it again if we could go back. We had no idea what the duration of the work and the questioning would do to us. I wonder now if it's destructive. How much doubt and anxiety can a person take before there is permanent damage to one's psyche?

I think about what we could contract out to get rid of some of the work. The drywall? The chimney? Todd said the drywall could cost $4,000. We can't bring ourselves to hire someone to do it for that price when we can do it ourselves. But can we do it ourselves? Can Todd's mind and inner peace deal with all this frustration, doubt, and questioning? I'm really afraid that he's reached his limit.

HINTS & TIPS:

- Closing in the gable ends of your log home can be challenging and a place to give some thought. Bear in mind that settling is more challenging to deal with in this area if you continue with log work to the peak of the roof. The roof pitch will change, and you must allow for settling around the rafters as it moves and slides. As a result, we solved this problem by building log trusses and framing out the openings.
- If you have an extra three or four hundred dollars, a generator would solve the problem of power if your lines are not yet in. Years ago, homeowners did not own generators like everyone does today. Only contractors had them.
- Don't quit. You can speak of quitting and vent to each other, but don't ever give up on your dream. Get some help (even if it's a psychological counselor or a therapist), take out a loan, hire someone, take a break and get away, but don't quit. Learning perseverance will help you handle many other challenges that life ahead has in store for you.

16
Pregnant

OUR FRIEND JOHN QUIMBY IS a forest entomologist who works for the Pennsylvania Bureau of Forestry. His principal activities involve researching and managing the gypsy moth infestation in our forests as well as other forest pests—including wood-boring insects. "Put the larvae in a film container with isopropyl alcohol and mail them to me," he says. "I'd be happy to check them out for you."

The news that comes back is very good. John is 99 percent sure that the adult of the larvae is called the white-spotted sawyer (*Monochamus scutellatus*). North of the Appalachian Mountains, their life cycle is two years, at the end of which they emerge to lay eggs in bark, and then the adult beetle dies. Since they will find no bark on the logs in our house, the eggs, if they are laid, will not survive. Seventy-five percent will die by natural occurrences anyway, John reports, one way being cannibalism. When their tunnels intersect, the larger larvae will eat the smaller. So, in two years, in June 1990, they will be trying to get out of the logs. The pictures of the adult beetle on the literature John sent us are not very attractive. Its black body is an inch long with another inch of antennae! It makes me cringe when I imagine them dropping out of the logs onto my sleeping baby and us at night. Perhaps we'll have to go for a trip in June 1990 to let them emerge in peace.

"Their exit holes are perfectly round," John says, "as opposed to their entrance holes and larvae galleries, which are oval. Look for the difference." On our sauna logs, sure enough, I find both kinds of holes.

Todd and I have decided to forgo fumigation. It's only one to two months of emerging beetles to deal with. No poisons. No money spent. I am glad we can live and let live, coexist for a while, and then the insects be on their way.

While John is checking out the larvae, Edgar Bachman is at our building site checking out our water situation. Edgar is a dowser who looks for underground water with a diving rod—a forked stick that bends downward when held over a source of water. Todd and I heard about him through our future neighbors who also got him to dowse their land. Dowsing isn't something that Todd and I strongly believe in, but neither are we disbelievers. We've just never been exposed to it to form an opinion. Edgar lives nearby and charges nothing for his service, so we have nothing to lose.

"Dowsing goes back to before Christianity," Edgar explains. "Egyptians drew dowsers on their walls as art. Most folks nowadays don't believe in it. If they can't do it, they don't believe in it." He walks around the woods by our house, fingering small branches until he finds a cherry tree. "I like a good hard wood," he says. He breaks off a branch where it forms a "Y" and grasps one side of the Y in each hand. Back and forth he walks in the woods, holding the stick outstretched in his hands. "See how it waves," he says. "The stick gently nods up and down. It's picking up spots, but they're not strong enough to draw. Water has to be there before the stick can go down. I can't make it happen."

Suddenly, the stick moves down to the ground. "I've found one," he exclaims. Then he moves back and dowses around the sides of that point to pick up the direction it is flowing.

"How do you tell how deep the water is?" I ask.

"A deep vein will start to grab the stick further away from where it kicks in," he says. He backs away from the vein to the "kick in point," where it "starts to go," and uses that distance as a guide.

"The depth of the water is usually about double that distance." He repeats the procedure from the opposite direction and at the same distance, the stick starts to pull down. "Your water is at about a hundred feet."

"A city water pipe is shallow," he goes on. "The stick will wait until the very last step and only then go down. It won't move gradually as it does in nature." Edgar locates the vein and Todd hammers in a wooden stake. It is at least a safe hundred feet from where the septic will go. "Hire a well driller who believes in dowsing," he instructs. "The disbelievers are thickheaded. They don't like to drill where a dowser says there's water."

Sixty-three-year-old Edgar used to be a well driller before he retired, as was his father and his father's father. "My dad began dowsing at the age of five. I began at nine. My dad used to say that it's in the mind, not the stick. The dowsers are using an unseen power, an energy connection. It's a gift that only some get, and the more you use it, the better it works." Edgar ignores the cold wind that is finding its way down his open neck and tells us dowsing stories.

"Some dowsers can find water on a map. It's called 'by proxy,' and it has nothing to do with a knowledge of topography or geography. Years ago, a dowser from Maine found water in Bermuda on a map, after the geologists said there wasn't any fresh water there. They drilled on his spot and found water sixty feet down and named the site after him. He was at a conference, and a 'smart-ass engineer' said, 'If you think you can find things so well, find the Kennedy half dollar that I've hidden.'

"The dowser never did that before, but he figured he's better try or he'd look bad, so he put the stick to his head and asked it questions. By process of elimination, he found it in the engineer's car trunk. He was just thrown off for a while, for he knew which state the engineer was from and the license plate on the car was not the same. The engineer then admitted that it was a rental car that he had picked up at the airport.

"Some dowsers dowse for oil. It's called 'wildcatting.' One man spent a year driving around in the back of a pickup and made $300,000. He said he was quitting after that. He was tired of being in the back of a truck all day.

"I once found a leak in a gas line by dowsing," Edgar tells us. "A woman I knew was complaining of a gas smell in her drinking water. I went over and dowsed where the vein got within fifty feet of the gas line. The gas company didn't want to do anything, because they had fixed it twice before, but they came out and saw me dowse and sure enough, once they dug, they found it.

"I once knew a man who spent $24,000 drilling wells, and they all came out dry. He finally asked me to come out and I found a vein right between two drilled holes only eighty feet down. Now, he's a believer.

"I read an article once that said scientists must stick together and not believe in dowsing. People are still dowsing, but I don't know of any young people doing it. The art should continue. Young people need to be shown how to do it and find out who has the gift."

Mick was so excited about Edgar coming to dowse that he took off work to come and watch. Todd wasn't a real strong believer, either, before he saw Edgar at work. By the end of the day, we are all pretty convinced. The stick moves a tiny bit for Mick but not nearly as strongly as it did for Edgar. And the next day Mick seems to have lost "the touch" altogether. When Todd tries, he says he *thinks* he can feel it pulling.

"Step backwards and dowse the vein with your eyes closed," I tell him. "If it works, the stick will go down on its own when you cross over it." He walks right over it without the stick ever flinching. He doesn't have the touch, either. And it's not something you can fake. I felt the stick when Edgar dowsed. I put my hand on it, next to his and I could feel the stick move all on its own, as though there was an inner force inside its bark. The real test will be when the drillers come.

Things have been going much better at the land and between Todd and me. Jobs have fallen into logical order, and I am spending more time helping Todd, for all my magazine deadlines have been met. We've also realized we must loosen up with one another. We need the confidence to believe that there will be periods of time where there will be spaces between us, but that these spaces will not last, nor are they a negative thing. Once I become pregnant, I will be involved in pregnancy things: reading books, writing in my journal, exercising. Things that will take my time away from Todd.

Before we were married, we attended a session called "Engaged Encounter" to teach us how to communicate with one another right from the start. The piece of advice that stuck strongest in my mind is to never let *anything* in your life together act as a wedge between you—not money, not a career, not even your children. Nothing must be allowed to interfere with the health of your relationship. I know that babies can act as a wedge between a couple. The husband must suddenly share his wife with another human being, long before they even enters the world. I feel very responsible for what will soon be growing inside of me. There is so much I want to learn and do. If Todd is not that interested, it could mean some difficult adjusting for us as a couple. These are the things that concern me. I don't want to lose what I've found from working with the logs all those years by my husband's side: shared sweat, shared joys and tears, shared accomplishments. This house-building project has put a strong foundation under us so that when the winds of change shift, we'll still be connected and not blow away.

There weren't any spaces between Todd and me this last week. We backpacked seventy miles up the barrier islands of the Outer Banks on the Cape Hatteras Beach Trail. It is the month of April, the first month we can attempt to conceive a child, because all the logs are up. I am determined to conceive at a special place.

By the ocean, Todd and I get very close again. On our first day hiking, he is enjoying himself so much he exclaims, "Let's go on more trips, honey." It is so good to hear! I hoped once I got him away from the building, he'd remember how much he loved having outdoor adventures. He relaxes, unwinds, and hopefully, we planted the seed that will turn we two into a family.

The first job to work on once we return from North Carolina is the chimney. It is late in the month of April and all fears of freezing temperatures are gone. We're using recycled bricks to build the chimney. Many are handmade and uneven from the molds. Others are hard brick from sidewalks that my Uncle Iggie tore up. We have a few different sizes and a few different thicknesses, which we use to our advantage to create a design. With our names and the date carved in, we make a solid concrete "brick" on the first-floor level. We stick a few seashells in the wet concrete "brick" for decoration. Right above this we build a brick shelf that extends out an inch or two for our ceramic "house angel" to sit on.

Some joints in the chimney are thick, others thin, but Todd makes sure that it is definitely plumb. It is not a static chimney, nor is it perfect; it is organic and earthy looking, and certainly beautiful. I was paging through our masonry books and read where it advised in bold letters: "DO NOT attempt to build a masonry chimney, brick or block, unless you are a master mason." Master masons we're not, although our foundation looks wonderful and our chimney so far looks the same. No wonder people are so afraid to attempt anything new on their own, with advice like this. Everyone thinks they must have professionals do the jobs. Years ago, a man had to know how to build and fix everything in his house and on his homestead. Now, he often knows how to do one thing in his life, his particular job, and many don't feel encouraged to enter another area of learning.

A few weeks have gone by and I've deduced that if I am not pregnant, there is something very wrong with my body. I have been starving since we came home from the Outer Banks; actually since the day after we made love in the dunes. My metabolism felt like it changed immediately, although my sister says I'm imagining it. Besides being famished all the time, I am tired and unusually cranky.

Up at the land today, we are working on the very top of the chimney. I stand high on the scaffolding, hugging the chimney, as I walk around it on the narrow planks. Gritty, dried mortar fragments make the boards slippery. I hold onto the roof lath and secure my hand before I take a step. I am a "hander" now: bricks, mortar, tape measure. I hand them up as Todd announces his need like a surgeon. Every time I bend to pick up something, I get dizzy and light-headed. I mix mortar and carry heavy buckets up the ladder, trying to keep my balance.

I accidentally drop wire mesh and empty water bottles and must make more trips down and up the ladder to fetch them. Todd calls for "special orders" and I must chisel bricks down to size. I wear safety glasses and a bandanna on my head for protection, but the mortar falls down the back of my neck from Todd up above. When I stand up quickly one time, I almost black out and as I grab for support, I complain loudly about the work conditions.

"It's good for the heart," he teases. "Now you know why I don't like it. It's no fun working up this high, is it? If it were down on the ground, building a chimney would be fun."

Back at the house, the UPS man drops off our seeds as we unload the truck. "Well, did it work on your trip?" he asks. I was so excited before we left for North Carolina that I told the world what *might* happen.

"I won't know for a week or so, but I sure feel pregnant."

"You know," he says, "I hear you can have that happen right here in Pennsylvania. You don't have to go all the way to North Carolina."

Once the chimney is complete, Todd can finally finish slating the roof, three months after the job began. I fill a fifteen-gallon plastic bucket with a half dozen slates. When I pull on the attached rope that goes up to a wheel that is chained to the ridgepole, the bucket rises and Todd grabs it, high on the scaffolding, and unloads it. These slates weigh seven pounds apiece. When the roof is complete, 3,000 slates will be nailed on. That's over ten tons of weight, not counting rafters, lath, etc. That's a lot of weight hoisted, too! When my planks are loaded with slate and supplies, I climb up to the collar tie of the truss and Todd climbs onto the roof.

I sit on the twelve-inch plank and wait to hand things up. It's cold up here. Wind blows through the openings. The temperature has dropped drastically while we've been working. Clouds move in and a few sprinkles fall. Todd is cold in his shorts. He wears a bright orange windbreaker with "Chris" embroidered on it in purple. It's my high school boyfriend's varsity jacket from fifteen years ago. Black tar splotches from coating the foundation are all over it. We carry it on the truck floor as a rag, but it comes in handy today as an extra layer of clothing.

I sit up here and look down at the open space of my future studio. I imagine the floor, my writing table, my easel. Todd says I'll have the best light in the house with my two skylights in the north roof. I hope to spend a lot of time up here. Suddenly I hear swearing and cursing coming through the roof hole. "Out of everything we've done on the house, this is the worst. I'll be up here all the time, crawling around, trying to fix this flashing."

The house is going to settle as the logs shrink. Every foot of vertical log will shrink three quarters of an inch. The chimney will not, however. It will look taller and be more exposed as the years go by, so Todd has to make flashing that will accommodate this radical shifting. Eight inches of copper flashing must overlap the brick chimney and the cricket (a wooden triangle that goes between the chimney and the roof) so snow and water do not collect in there and leak. The copper flashing is recycled from the slate roof we salvaged, and Todd is having a hard time getting such big, overlapping pieces to lie flat. He's all alone up there. He'll be losing his helper on even more jobs if I'm pregnant. I read in my childbirth books that I need to avoid any job that creates fumes or threatens the respiratory tract, such as cleaning the mildewed logs with bleach, sanding wallboard, and painting.

My menstrual cycle is two weeks late and because of that, and how sick I'm feeling, I am sure I am into my second month of pregnancy. Up at the land, my new normal position is lying on a nylon webbed chaise lounge, because I feel so sick. Todd moves it from one room to the next as he works so I can keep him company. Every now and then the nausea passes, and I can lend a hand. Today, I'm handing up fifteen-foot boards of tongue-and-groove yellow pine for the second floor. We ordered a truckload from a lumberyard but needed about thirty more boards that Todd had to fetch himself.

"I had a little adventure getting these here," Todd says as he grabs one end of the board from me. "I tied the boards on the top of the truck's roof rack. They extended over the hood and made the whole load top heavy. It's twenty-five miles from the lumberyard to here. In the meantime, the ropes loosened up considerably from the boards shifting around. When I came down off Hawk Mountain, the whole load leaned forward. When I applied my brakes on that first sharp curve, the wood slipped off the rack and shot right over the front of the truck. I was plowing them down the mountain! As soon as it happened, I stopped the truck and cleared the road as quickly as I could. Jim Brett from Hawk Mountain Sanctuary drives by right then and asks what had happened and if I need help. I told him a deer ran out in front of me and made me slam on my brakes and lose my load."

"Why did you tell him that?" I ask, laughing.

"I didn't want him to think I didn't know how to tie lumber down!"

As we had anticipated, there are some spaces opening up between Todd and I over this baby. This evening, Todd was sitting on the sofa just staring. When I ask what is wrong, he blurts out,

"It seems like I don't matter much anymore. After Cape Hatteras, I feel like that was the end of me and my wife. Now it's you and the baby. You said to me, 'I'm not going to take care of you like I have been. You're going to have to fend for yourself.'"

That was my half-joking answer when he acted helpless and needed me to tell him what to snack on this evening.

"That was partially true, honey," I tell him. "You will be on your own more. In my last month of pregnancy, I'll be tired from carrying thirty extra pounds around. When the baby comes, I'll be breastfeeding every two hours, I'll be up a few times a night, and I'll be tired from that."

"It already feels like a wedge is coming between us," Todd admits. "It seems like you never want to go to the land. You're just into your walks, your exercise, and your diet."

"I need your support with this baby," I tell Todd. "Come for walks *with* us. Read some of these books. Understand what is happening to my body and the baby." I hug and kiss him and tell him that he is not alone in these feelings. "Don't be scared. It's just going to be different. I'll always be your buddy. I'll always be your best friend. That's not going to change. We're just going to have more love in our lives."

We must learn to trust our marriage and believe it is strong enough to pull us through these changes and come out closer to one another.

The next morning, the shrill sound of the telephone wakes us up. "This is Phares Fry calling. We're coming to drill your well."

"When?" Todd asks.

"This morning. Is the access clear? The men are ready to leave."

We jump out of bed, get dressed, and pack up, for we still must cut a few saplings down so the big rig can back up to the stake that we pounded into the ground after dowsing. It poured hard last night, and the ground is very wet, much too wet for the normal building site where there is excavated dirt everywhere. We're surprised that they're even going to try. Apparently, they're hoping that a wooded site will be dry enough to drive on.

Five minutes on the site proves them wrong. As soon as the truck backs off our shale road and into the woods, it sinks 1.5 feet. They jack the monster truck up, first one side and then the other, tilting precariously on two little jacks. It makes Todd and me back away.

"Did it ever tilt over?" I ask.

"Close!" they answer.

They throw thick oak planks down on the ground and try to run the wheels on them. Over and over they try. Sometimes the wheels spit the planks out into the air. We lay firewood sections down side by side to gain some height. One man keeps getting his whole body under the suspended truck to arrange lumber. It could crush him like a fly, but I guess he trusts it. The truck moves back about two feet with every attempt.

"We have no place else to go so we may as well keep trying."

One of the drillers is a dowser, too, and he finds water with his stick at the exact spot that Edgar Bachman found it. They take every measure to get the rig directly over the exact spot. They work at moving the truck back to the stake in the ground for two hours. We are glad we are not paying them by the hour. The truck has a bubble on it so they know when the truck is level and plumb, for the drill will not work otherwise. I carry my lawn chair out and get comfortable, prepared to watch throughout the day with my box of crackers for nausea. Different-colored dusts shoot out of the holes: yellow, then ruddy colored, then brown, then gray. It's all Tuscarora sandstone, what these Appalachian Mountains are made of. The two men drill straight through lunch. They eat their sandwiches and bananas while they work and chew tobacco for dessert.

One driller, whose plaid flannel shirt cannot quite cover his big belly, is jolly and answers all my questions. The other looks old and tired, like he has breathed too much rock dust over the years. He works the shovel, keeping the drill area free of dirt, and helps divert the gray mud water from the area. I wonder how many landowners sit and watch the whole process from a lawn chair. At about 120 feet they hit water. Close enough, Edgar! For the first time in seven years, we can entertain the thought of running water. Well, we *almost* have it. A few jobs must be completed before we can actually see the liquid running out of a hose. One is the electrical work, for the pump is run on electric.

Our friend Scott Cooper, who built and wired his whole house, works for four hours helping Todd hook up our meter box and main breaker. When the electrical inspector comes to check the work, he opens the panel and abruptly says, "*Wrong!* All three wires are hooked on the wrong terminals. If the electric company hooked power to this, it would blow your house up." We doubt this. Maybe the wall. Maybe just the panel box. It's a strong house. He screws the lid back on the box and says, "That will be sixty-seven dollars. Call me when it's right." His inspection lasts only two minutes!

"Must we pay you *another* sixty-seven dollars when you come back?" I ask in horror.

"No. I'll be easy on you," he says.

As it turns out, Scott's house is serviced by a different electric company and his box gets hooked up differently than ours. It takes Todd all of five minutes to switch the wires. The inspector probably had the right tool in his truck for either him or us to correct the job on the spot. We really don't care how many times he has to come back. *We just want power!*

Days come and go. Ditches are dug for electric and water. The well pipe is laid, the pump installed, and the electric put in. Todd and I unravel the telephone cord and lay it in the same ditch, fighting protruding tree roots as I walk down the ditch toward the creosoted pole. I hold the curling wire down with my foot while Todd drops a few shovelfuls of soil on it to keep it flat. He had entertained the idea of backfilling the ditches by hand but Paul German, our excavator, just laughed and said, "It will take my machine three quarters of an hour to do the job and you two weeks." Todd succumbed. He's getting smarter. Not everything is worth doing yourself, just because you can.

Once the electric and the water are in, we can finally rent a power washer and clean the mildew off our logs. We cannot put any drywall up downstairs until this soaking-wet job is finished. I scrubbed the mildew and dirt off our sauna without Todd's help and know the magnitude of work we're up against. After having been exposed to so many rains, some of our house logs are black with mildew.

We pick up the huge machine at a rental store and roll it off the truck on ramps.

I turn the washer on while Todd positions himself, wand in hand. I next turn on the kerosene burner to heat the water. Todd gets soaked but the warm water that's drenching him keeps him from getting cold. I push buttons on and off for him. It's quite amazing to watch the mildew disappear so easily in a single stroke. Supposedly, there is 500–600 pounds of pressure coming out of the nozzle, but Todd can stick his hand in front of it painlessly. He places the nozzle an inch or two from the log and actually blasts a thin layer of wood off the logs. Fuzzy pulp lies on the ground and on the inside flooring, washed off by the water. The logs feel furry to the touch, but they are much brighter than they were before and that is all we care about. Todd aims his wand at the fungus growing between two logs and it blasts out and sticks to his wet face, hair, and skin, along with the wood pulp. He is a mess.

All through the day, Todd takes very little time out to rest. He wants to finish the whole house, inside and out, before the day is over, so we can return the machine to the rental store and only pay for one day's use. By late afternoon, the burner stops working, and Todd freezes from the cold water. The logs also aren't getting very clean anymore, and he is beat.

By 7:00 p.m., the machine starts to sputter and shuts off. Out in the open field, by the "shaving factory," the sky has grown black with storm clouds. Todd is concerned about getting electrocuted, for the electric light cords that are run out to our panel box are lying in the water.

The machine instructions say you are only to operate it if your electric is ground faulted, which would trip the electricity off if it gets wet, which ours is not. Our outlet is still hot. Daylight has faded. I get a flashlight out of the glove compartment and hold it to a log to help Todd see. It's getting ridiculous to continue. He's exhausted. He's hypothermic. If we break this expensive machine we may have to repair or replace it. And now an electrical storm is rolling in. "Let's get out of here!" I announce. We leave the last room incomplete, pack up the machine in the pickup truck, and drive home in the pouring rain, cleaning off the power washer as we go.

It's June and my morning sickness, which lasted much of the day, has finally subsided, and I have once again, joined the workforce. We are now ready to begin the interior finishing work: floors, walls, windows, and doors. Our tentative moving-in date is scheduled for Thanksgiving weekend. Our baby is due in mid-January, and we'd like a good month to get settled. Todd is against bringing this baby into a cold house. But if we can't finish enough of our home to move in by Thanksgiving, we've decided to stay where we are, in the drafty national park service house.

Some days, when progress is good, it looks like we may get it done before the winter. On bad days, even the following spring seems unrealistic. We've been at it now for over three years, and completion never seems to draw any closer. More and more jobs appear before Todd's eyes with every inch of progress he makes. He crawled onto the sofa with me the other day while I rested and said, "I'm tired of it, honey. I don't want to build this house the rest of my life. I'd like to move on and do something else with my life someday."

"You will," I chuckle. "It will be over soon." Five months remain until Thanksgiving. Will we be carving our turkey in this cold house, or in the warmth of our new log home?

HINTS & TIPS:

- It is up to each home builder how many of the individual construction jobs they plan to take on—if they like doing the jobs, enjoy learning new skills, and if they can afford to subcontract them out or not. Subbing them out does not always guarantee that it will save time or that it will get done better. Professional contractors know where they can cut corners and still be structurally sound. The homeowner may do a better job themselves and can also save money in doing it themselves.

- You could contract out finishing jobs like the plumbing, the drywall, electrical, etc., but Todd's philosophy is, "I do every job myself. I *can* do every job myself and I need to do every job myself. That's the kind of person that I am. Knowing how to do all these jobs and having all these skills gives me a better understanding of how things work, and that's very important to me, that knowledge base."
- The white-spotted sawyers remained in our logs, grinding away and chewing, for about two years. They often kept us awake at night as they chewed tunnels in our bedroom logs. Todd even tried to inject borax into their tunnels to squelch them with the syringe we use to flush out the cat's wounds, but to no avail. The chewing intensified in the humid summer months when the moisture of the logs increased but quieted down when the woodstove was cranking in the winter. In a few years, the insects finally emerged in the beetle stage and looked for tree bark to lay their eggs on. Finding none, they moved on or we squashed them. Our entomologist friend assured us years back that they would not be a problem and when it was all said and done, it was true. They could not have possibly eaten enough of our massive logs to have done any structural damage. Their memory remains, however, in their oval entrance holes and their round exit holes—just one part of our log building adventure.

17
Grand Finale

For a professional electrician, wiring a log house can be a nightmare, let alone for a log builder with little experience. The interior of half of our house is solid log with no studded walls in which to run wires. Todd wanted me to decide where I wanted sinks, the tub, the refrigerator, very early in the construction when we only had three rounds of logs on the building and it still looked more like a shallow corral than a house. Todd didn't even have the truss and roof design figured out at that point, but I had to decide on room layout, furnishings, and patterns of traffic. The height of three rounds of logs is the height at which floor outlets should be, so at that point in the building, he augured one hole through the third log down to the basement and another one perpendicular to that for the outlet. Then the fourth round of logs covered up the top of that hole forever.

Now that we're ready to wire, Todd's first step is to plunge cut with the tip of his chain saw into the wood around the outlet. It's tricky work because an overcut won't be covered by the outlet plate. Then he smooths out the edges with a hand chisel.

We position light switches in the log part of the house by doorways so that their wires can be hidden in a cut sawed out for the doorjambs. Because the logs will settle, the doorjambs cannot be nailed directly to the house, for the logs need to be able to move. (Nor can the steps or the interior studded walls be attached!) Todd has to cut a spline and place a floating two-by-four in it and nail the jamb to that. This cut is a good place to hide his electrical wires for the switches.

In order to wire the second floor, we need to find a wall common to the first floor. This is difficult because much of the upstairs is open loft. All second-floor wires must be run to that solitary wall, which in this case is one little space. Todd must do difficult and time-consuming jobs like drilling holes through the end truss logs to hide his wires. It's no wonder that the wiring is taking weeks and weeks. As he gets finished with one circuit, however, he guides me through the house, demonstrating the magic of how flicking a plastic switch can activate electrical lights. He is continually amazed and very pleased with his work, as being an electrician had been his second career choice in high school, after woodworking.

Another reason his wiring is turning into a forever job is because he is continually interrupted to work on other aspects of the building. Dave Walp and I have been working on laying sheets of plywood for subfloors ever since Todd began wiring. Dave measures and cuts, I take Todd's Milwaukee drill and depress the drywall screws into the plywood. But now our work has come to a standstill. All that's left to

subfloor is the living room, but we cannot do that until Todd builds the steps to the second floor, which lead from that room. When he had laid the second floor, he merely left a hole for the steps with no preplanning or premeasuring as to how many steps he'd need or how high he'd need to make the risers. Never having built steps before, he assumed he could figure it out once he arrived at that point in the building.

As it turns out, the space is not large enough for straight stairs and instead, he must make pie-shaped steps to get around the corner. The only book we have that illustrates any type of stair building simply mentions pie-shaped steps, states that you should not build them, and then—in typical fashion—moves on.

With the help of Todd's father, Dale, who is also gifted in woodworking, Todd eventually figures it out and builds a set of beautiful and safe steps out of scrap maple boards and pine planks recycled from crates. However, since the house is still settling, and the steps cannot be attached at the top and the bottom, the finished steps are just pushed into place and nailed down. The top step will get smaller as the logs shrink and dry and the second floor drops lower. It sounds difficult and it certainly can be destructive if you don't allow for settling. We heard of one couple's house whose kitchen cabinets were screwed onto the log walls at various places and resulted in broken cabinets as the logs shrank and moved. With a Scandinavian scribed fit log home, this concept must always be taken into consideration. But with some practice, it becomes second nature. Once the house is complete, Todd will need to crank down the four upright posts holding up our porch and sunroom (one of which is our carved girl with the knots in the right places). They posts have giant screw pins in their bottoms and for five years, the house will settle as the logs dry, shrink, and settle.

While the steps are underway, Todd realizes he must stop and build the built-in bookshelf that fits inside and along the steps. He will need to hide wiring inside the shelf's wall and install an outlet, so it's back to carpentry for a while. He gets frustrated by all these jobs he hasn't figured time for, but they must all still get done eventually. He does make progress, though, contrary to how he sometimes feels.

At about the same time our buddy Mick goes off to hike the entire Appalachian Trail (for the second time), Dave Walp returns on weekends to help build. He was called back to work so he can only come Saturdays and Sundays, but those two days are so helpful. One wonderful worker replaces the next. Dave has experience doing many of the conventional house-building jobs we are now doing. Suggestions flow freely. Todd takes some suggestions while others merely drift through the air. Dave is good-natured, though, not pushy. And he seems to know that Todd has a mind of his own when it comes to building his house.

The flooring that Dave and I have been laying down has an interesting history. The four-inch tongue-and-groove yellow pine that is in the hallway is the floor that we ripped out of a picnic pavilion that our logger Randy Bloc showed us years ago. Our living room floor is made of wide pine boards from an attic in a house that my Uncle Iggie tore down. When my girlfriend Annie stopped up the other day to check on our progress, she commented about the pine floor. "I remember seeing that floor as a pile of junk wood with nails sticking out of it and broken ends. I just couldn't see how that pile of kindling could turn into a living room floor, but it really is beautiful."

It makes economic sense to salvage usable building materials. It is more sustainable, and it gives our home a magical feel. Thinking of what occurred within the walls of those different buildings and the people that lived and walked there so many years ago makes us happy that we're saving them from a dump.

The whole month of August is dedicated to drywalling. Putting up sheets of four-by-eight-foot drywall isn't an exceedingly difficult job to learn or do, but Todd has to put them up on a forty-five-degree ceiling, twenty-five feet in the air. Most log home builders use two-by-six-inch pine decking for the ceiling. We want to get as much light into our home as possible, so we are putting drywall up and painting it off-white. That little bungalow that we lived in when we were first married sat in a hollow in an evergreen forest on the north side of a hill. We needed all of the lights on in the house in order to see, even at noon. We want our log house to be bright inside. Log home interiors can lean toward the dark side naturally, and we have enough wood in the house as it is with log walls, wood floors, and wooden furniture.

Dave has become Todd's helper since drywalling isn't a good job for a pregnant woman whose balance is a little tipsy. Todd did get me to help put in our three-by-six-foot stained-glass window high in our truss however, for no one else was around. The wooden frame and an additional pane of safety glass pushed its weight to almost one hundred pounds. I had to stand on a twelve-inch-wide plank eight feet in the air, pull on a rope to get it up, and then guide it into the hole in the truss wall. My head was swaying from the height and the exertion.

Spackling the drywall isn't a bad job. Instead of sanding, which is the part everyone hates, at my girlfriend's suggestion, we choose the wet sponge method of smoothing out the spackling. This enables me to help on this monumental job, which lasts throughout the month of September.

Over Labor Day weekend, we take time out to drive to Maine and climb Mt. Katahdin for recreation and to do research for a magazine article I'd been contracted to write. When we return home, we must put off building a little longer yet, to harvest our organic garden. We press grapes and apples for juice and cider, make sauerkraut and peach preserves, can tomatoes and freeze beans for a full week. Meanwhile, the Thanksgiving goal for completion looms closer.

I help when I can on the first and second floors and leave the ceiling for Todd. Pretty soon the walls are all finished and painted with an off-white latex paint provided by Todd's brother Brendt, who had worked at a Sherwin-Williams store. We buy gallons of discontinued paint—off-white, eggshell, bone, and cream color—mix them all together and have enough of the same color to cover all our interior walls and ceilings.

The only two floors that need finishing work are the tile floor in the kitchen and bath, and the parquet floor in our bedroom. The cabinet factory that Todd used to work at threw all their scrap wood away—good quality, sanded hardwood. On his lunch breaks, he used to saw scraps into six-inch squares and cut a groove in them for a spline. He kept choosing larger lunch boxes until finding an insulated, zippered picnic bag that could hold the three-square feet that he was cutting per night.

Todd cuts splines for the parquet squares out of old sheets of paneling from a house my uncle tore down. When he hammers the first spline into a groove with a rubber mallet, it splinters and breaks apart into hairy layers. Masonite would work much better than this inferior material, but he can't see buying it when we have this, even if it is junk. Todd is swearing right at the start of the job and already doesn't want to do it.

"We're just in the figuring-out stage," I say. "Let's get the hang of it." After I plane the edges of the paneling, it goes into the groove much better. I drill two nail holes and stack up my squares in two piles: horizontals on one side, verticals on the other. Within a few days, the parquet floor is complete.

One of the most unconventional aspects of building a Scandinavian scribed log house is that the windows and doors are hung last. It is best to let the logs air dry as long as possible, for as soon as the interior of the house is heated, the logs begin to dry out unevenly, faster inside than out. As a result, most of our interior finishing work is complete and people who come up to see what we're doing can still walk through the entire house unhindered, as though it were public property. This really bothers Todd and me. I'm not excited about cleaning black sole marks off floors or dirty fingerprints off walls before we even move in.

While Todd cuts jambs, I scrape the glass of the newly painted windows. All the windows in our house are recycled, except for the skylights. The six-foot stained-glass window in the living room was a steal at $300. One day before we were even married, we stopped at a stained-glass store in York, Pennsylvania, and saw six beautiful church windows. All were priced alike. All were broken, dirty, and in need of repair, except one.

"Why is that one is such good shape?" I asked the owner.

"A man was going to buy it. He took it out to his truck and dropped it and asked me to repair it. He hasn't paid for the window or the repairs and it's been months!"

It was clear the man was disturbed. "If we give you $300 in cash right now, can we buy *this* window?" He was quick to say yes, and we went back to Todd's parents' house for their truck, for they lived only a mile away. Todd was not too sure of the purchase. I needed to talk him into it. This was the first piece of salvage we gathered and at that point, we had no design of any kind for our house.

"For this price," I told him, "we can design the house around the window," which is exactly what we did. There are aquamarine, rose, lemon-yellow, and lime-green pieces of glass in the window. We put it high in the truss on the east side of the house where it catches the morning light, bathing the whole kitchen and dining room area in warm, golden hues.

That was the beginning of our salvage scavenging. As years went by, we gathered quite a collection. We rented a house twice the size of the little bungalow we lived in to store it all. It was great fun, collecting free "junk" that we had saved from destruction. Thinking creatively about how to use it in our new home brought us even more pleasure.

The windows that I'm scraping came from a huge public sale of used building supplies that the nearby Kempton Community Center hosts every spring. Thirteen auctioneers are working at one time. There are dozens of rows of all kinds of stuff and you find yourself running back and forth, trying to judge if the crowd is close to the spot where the piece of junk you want is. The local Amish do it right. They send their older children out separately to bid and give them definite limits on how high to go. The arched windows that will go on either side of our stained-glass church window were the first thing I ever bid.

"*Five dollars!*" I yell to start the bid.

"You should start at a quarter!" Todd reprimands me. Luckily, no one wants them, and I have no other bidders and got three windows for five dollars, still a good price.

We read in a design book of energy-efficient homes that one third of a home's light is lost through a window screen. (If you add two more strands to a screen, it would be dark.) We aren't willing to give up *any* light. Plus, in order to use recycled windows efficiently, we permanently caulk them into place, along with storm windows, to make them double paned. Underneath the recycled window, Todd builds a vent about ten inches high—the height to which a window is normally opened. It has a screen for the summer, and an insulated foam faceboard for the winter. We use this design on all of our recycled windows, making them energy as well as cost efficient.

I was going to make some stained-glass windows for our home but when we find some at an antique mart for forty dollars apiece, we decide I don't really have the time or the desire to begin a new hobby. Our front door on the south side of the house has panes of beautiful beveled glass and two beveled glass side panels. We ripped it out of a church rectory that my uncle was tearing down in the coal regions of Pennsylvania. One panel was broken, costing twenty-five dollars to replace. It's distressing to think that almost $900 of beveled glass was all going to be destroyed by a wrecking ball.

After all the tedious work, there are fun jobs left like choosing which doorknobs go best on which doors: white porcelain, brown marbleized, crystal, or brass . . . all recycled, all possessing character as well as beauty. We like these details. We get excited seeing the house turn into a creative expression of ourselves. Although these material things aren't really important in and of themselves, we get a lot of joy out of creating beauty, working with our hands, and turning "junk" into useful things.

After working late, we go out in the night and look at our house that is lit up from the inside. This is the very first time we've worked late enough to need the lights on. That beveled glass door creates such a grand, elegant entrance. On the east side, warm color glows through the six-foot stained glass window.

"Let's go out to the 'shaving factory' and walk down our lane as though we are strangers approaching our house." We hold hands and look at our house, seeing it as if it were the first time. "Looks like someone is at home," I comment, as we approach the house.

"Such a fine beautiful house," Todd says. "The owners must be really proud."

Just a few jobs are left now: sanding and oiling the wood floors and the one big job of laying our tile floors. Three weeks remain until Thanksgiving, and it looks like we'll make it. Those things necessary in order to move in are nearly finished. We still won't have plumbing, kitchen cabinets, or bookshelves, but those things will come in their time. Although having plumbing is considered a necessity in most homeowners' eyes, after years of living without, we can wait a little longer for that "luxury!" The thought of moving out of our old drafty house saddens me a bit, silly as that may sound. I will miss being situated right by the Appalachian Trail, our bountiful orchard, the view of the ridge, and the open field where we watch hawks soar. The old house has felt like home for so long: four years.

When Todd was feeling frantic and pressured about building, I almost got him to agree to stay here for the winter and the birth. I wonder if part of me needs to have something stable in my life in the midst of this roller-coaster ride. They say you should never move when you're about to have a baby. Too much change. There will be time though, before the baby comes, for us to get settled; time to make the house feel cozy and look familiar. It isn't like the new house is unfamiliar. We've been going there for nearly four years. But it always seemed like a place to visit, a place to go to work, a place to leave. I still get excited to pack up work and come back to this old house. Once all our things are out though, it will feel cold and empty like my mother's house after she died.

Todd wakes up very early for work now. He is primed. "Full speed ahead," he says. He is into his work, not pressured or stressed in the least, for he says, "It's really happening." He says that a lot. Almost every day.

Dave Walp has been laid off from work and has been coming nearly every day to help wrap things up. He's doing time-consuming work like putting up trim. Todd's parents and even his aunt and uncle came up to wash windows, buff floors, and sand log ends. Only one big job remains: the tile floor.

This morning, Todd is acting separate and distant from me. It is the day we pick up the diamond saw from the rental store to cut tile and the day our hiking friend, Dick Potteiger, comes to show us how to do it. We went to three stores last night, looking for the right size of notched trowel for spreading mortar but found none. Before breakfast, Todd goes out to his shop to grind bigger spaces into a trowel he already has. "Wear your raincoat and your rubber boots," I yell to him, for it is pouring out.

He does not and as a result, soaks his cotton sweatshirt through to his skin. When I ask him what he wants for breakfast, he snaps at me saying, "I don't care!" and says nothing else the rest of the morning. When I ask him what his problem is, he says he's tired of hearing me tell him to put things on when he hates raincoats. Seven months pregnant, and I'm feeling weepy.

"I don't want my toast and eggs. You can have them," I say.

"You're always hungry," he says, "What's the matter?"

"I hate when you don't talk to me. If there is something wrong, then share it with me."

"I'm worried," he says. "1 don't know how to mix the mortar. I don't know how to cut tile. I don't know how to snap the chalk lines. I don't know how to do any of it."

I know, of course, that the tile is the problem, but he needs to share it in the open. I rub his arm and say, "Your buddy Dick is coming.

You're not doing it alone. He knows a lot. He tiled his own house. Together you'll be able to figure it out. You've figured everything else out up to this point. Have some confidence in yourself. You act like you're going to war. You're only going to lay tile."

He smiles, but his eyes suddenly glisten with tears, ever so slightly. Oh, my sweetheart, I think to myself. I'll go up there in an hour and everything will be moving along just fine.

And so it is. They have the first few rows of tiles already laid out and in place when I arrive. Chalk lines have been snapped as reference points, adhesive has been laid, and three to four rows of tile have been set in place. Dick runs the diamond saw that works like a radial arm saw, except instead of the blade moving, you move the table that the tile sits on, into the blade. It is very noisy and wet, for it sprays water on the blade to keep it cool. I help out by placing the tiles down, making sure the space in between them is fairly uniform, as we have no spacers for hexagon tiles to measure against. I tap them into the mortar with a rubber mallet to set them. Todd keeps me supplied with mortar and measures end tiles for Dick to cut. In one day, we have 225 square feet laid.

The next day Dave comes to help grout. We sponge a film of Murphy's Oil Soap on each tile top to keep the grout from soaking into the unglazed quarry tile. We then trowel the grout in between the tiles and fill in the joints. In a couple of hours, we wipe the tiles off with rags and sponges. The water turns the color of the brick red grout quickly and one person is kept busy just filling up the water bucket at the hose.

We're laying 315 total square feet of tile in the kitchen, dining room, and bath. We can afford it because we went right to the factory where the tiles are made and purchased them at a considerable savings. I called a distributor with questions, and a young boy who was filling in answered the phone. I asked where they bought them, and he gave me the factory's name and phone. "Do you have seconds?" I asked, when I called. Yes, they did. They mailed us the showroom's catalog, and we picked our favorites from the tiles they were running at the time. The seconds have miniscule flaws. Maybe a dark speck, or a slightly curved down corner—such inconspicuous flaws that many stores buy them and sell them as firsts, they told us. Because we dealt with the factory, our price was almost half the price of the distributor. We could tell this wasn't normally done—laypeople off the street dealing with the factory—for every time I reached the secretary, she wanted to know what company I was from. The factory is the same driving distance as the distributor, so it didn't make sense to pay almost double. We bought our grout and our adhesive there, too, in big fifty-pound bags at an unbelievable savings, instead of the tiny "kits" they sell at the retail stores. And on top of that, the manager sent us detailed instructions on how to lay the tiles and answered my dozens of questions, unhurried, and with extreme kindness. Our last major construction job has turned into recreation.

After my mother died, Thanksgiving dinner with my siblings came to an end. Todd's family never made much of the holiday, so it was up to us to decide whether we ate turkey lunch meat sandwiches from the deli or a full feast with all the trimmings. We became the new hosts. We didn't want to break with tradition, moving or not, so we left our old house in pretty much the same state for the holiday, even though we will move the very next day.

Todd's dad and brother Brendt spent the night after the holiday and helped us pack dishes, silverware, and glass jars of food before we went to bed. It is cold on moving day. Sixteen degrees. The men wake up before dawn from the chill and try to start a fire in the wood cookstove by sleepily throwing a too-big log on a near-dead fire. Already last night, the house no longer looked like home and on this cold morning, it does not feel warm like a home, either.

A very dear old friend from my childhood, Annie Nawaczinski, and her husband, Joey, arrive with their pickup truck to help move. While the men carry loads, Annie and I take down pictures, unscrew shelves, and pack boxes, staying one step ahead of the movers. I am large with child by now, and my oversized insulated suit finally fits me. I have to rest often for I get easily fatigued from the packing. But all the chairs are gone! I drop my heavy body into a corner on the floor, but Annie never skips a beat.

Up at the log house, she unwraps the contents of our hutch and antique ice box, rolls out our handmade braided wool rug, and positions the furniture as I direct.

"I won't be able to sleep tonight unless this one area, at least, looks and feels like home for you," she says. We can't talk anyone into staying for supper. They all want to give us time alone.

While Todd works on hooking up the woodstove, I spoon large servings of leftover turkey dinner onto a casserole and pop it into the oven. We sit at our round oak pedestal table that Todd made, with the casserole between us on a folded newspaper as a hotplate; no dishes, but two large spoons and a communal glass of water between us. We take a hand to say grace.

For the first time, our moving, exhausted bodies have stopped. We look around at the log walls and realize where we are. Our hands tighten and our eyes fill with tears. We are so grateful for this beautiful house, for all that we learned, and that no one was injured.

Our bed is not yet assembled. There's just the mattress thrown on the floor, but we dive in and sleep soundly for the very first night we've ever spent "up at the land."

Waking comes slow. Our eyelids separate with the down comforter nestled around our necks. Warm sunlight is hitting the massive, honey-colored logs above our heads. When we trace its origin, we see brilliant light streaming through the beveled glass door, throwing rainbows all around the kitchen. A golden glow covers the floor from the stained-glass window high in the truss. Through the windows, we see the bare oak trees and the graceful white pines swaying in the morning breeze. We've never experienced a morning like this, in this house. We lay holding each other for a long, long time, taking in the beautiful sight before us. We do not speak. There are no words to say, but we are both feeling the same thing. Our log house has finally become a home.

HINTS & TIPS:
(Advice for Salvage Collectors)

- We would have never been able to build a home this inexpensively had we not incorporated salvage. The time it takes to acquire salvage, as well as the creativity necessary to reuse it, must be weighed against the price of buying new. And working with salvage has its limitations. It can require much more skill, and it forces you to think creativity. Perfection is not always achieved. The attitude of "learning to live with things as they are" must sometimes be embraced.

- We went to public sales that we saw advertised in the newspaper. Anticipating a need—someday—for floors, doors, window jambs, kitchen cabinets, bookshelves, stairs, etc., we bought up all the lumber we could get our hands on at a good price.

- As we got more involved with salvaging, our vision changed—how we looked at things and what we looked *at* changed. When we drove in rural areas, we looked for old barns or sheds that were falling down but still contained good wood. We'd notice a pile of bricks in someone's yard, left over from a project and then ask if they had a use for them or would they be willing to part with the old building materials. Whenever we traveled, we'd stop at every junkyard or secondhand store along our way.

- Another thing to keep in mind is that just because an object was used for one thing, does not mean it cannot be used for something different. For example, old tongue-and-groove flooring can be used to make wonderful kitchen cabinets. A smooth interior door works just as well as a worktable or a desktop. We found some ¼-inch plate glass at a local junkyard that was used as the jewelry and make-up counters at a now-defunct department store. We bought them for a dollar apiece and used them as long vertical windows.

- You must get out of the mindset that new is always better. Our living room floor was made out of old wide pine boards that were ripped out of a house. Not only would it be very difficult to find a source of new wide pine boards, they would be very expensive, and they wouldn't have that warm patina from years of use. The same is true of our solid five-paneled wood interior doors, whose paint was stripped off. Their beauty far exceeds that of any hollow-core door used today.
- When you're collecting salvage, you have to leave your timidity behind. Some treasures fall into your lap, but most have to be discovered, and then inquired about. You might become friendly with some local contractors and offer to buy their leftover supplies at a fraction of the cost. The important thing to remember is to always have your antennae up—looking, searching for materials and objects that you could offer a second life to. Networking is a major ingredient in successful salvaging. Get the word out to everyone that you are in the market for used building materials. Remember that besides saving yourself a lot of money, and creating a uniquely beautiful house, you will be doing something noble and beneficial for your community and for the earth by saving it from the landfill. There are now used building supply stores in some communities as well as salvage stores, which of course are not free, but the work was already done for you.
- Public sales are a good place to find used windows, for example. It seems everyone has old windows lying around that were replaced with more efficient ones. Out of the forty-plus windows in our entire house, we only paid for three new windows. They are the skylights in my studio and one over the living room. We used techniques from passive solar home designs to make our salvaged windows energy efficient.
- In our log home, we have seventeen doors, including two homemade Victorian screened doors. Of the seventeen, eleven were made almost entirely from salvage or wood acquired through

bartering. The other six were free. As a matter of fact, many other doors were picked up and used as outside picnic tables, coal bins, or used to stack firewood off the ground. Along with those free doors came the hinges. Not a single hinge was purchased for our doors—thirty-five in total, some ornately decorated. Doorknobs, rim locks, and latch sets also came along with most of the doors. Black, white, and brown porcelain knobs, glass crystal knobs, and a solid brass latch set have new homes in our doors.

- Wood is perhaps the most easily adaptable and salvageable material there is. Having the tools to work with wood will allow you endless possibilities to reuse your finds. A whole shop full of tools could be purchased and paid off in little time by avoiding buying new lumber and using the tools to adapt your free lumber to your building needs. In the end, when your building projects are over, if that is possible, you will have a shop full of tools, which could be resold if you find that woodworking is not your cup of tea.
- You can often find weathered wood if you have the opportunity to dismantle a building. Old barns provide large quantities. The building's age, how the weather hit the walls, and the kind of wood it is all determine its weathered look. Using it on walls in place of paneling or drywall opens up many possibilities, like running it in vertical or horizontal lines or using mosaic patterns to make sunburst designs on the wall. In certain situations where the boards are too weatherworn or paint makes them unappealing, they can still be used by flipping them to their backside. The board will have a much newer look. Resawing old barn boards will open up fresh edges which can be difficult to match with the weathered look, so use foresight before cutting.
- Salvaged joists, rafters, and beams add up to monetary savings on your building projects. Because it is usually full-sized dimensions, as opposed to today's lumber store lumber, it is stronger and often better quality. Scarce lumber like old chestnut boards and logs can be found in old buildings and resawn into lumber for resale at a high market value.

Epilogue: 2020

When most people see our log home in person for the first time, they are astonished, especially upon learning that Todd and I built it ourselves from raw trees. It looks like a massive undertaking, and, after reading this book, you will likely agree that it was indeed. But in hindsight, after three decades cycled past, we no longer think of it as an extraordinary feat. It was just our life at the time, a goal that we set, which we worked hard to accomplish.

Soon after we completed its construction, we birthed two children, Sierra and Bryce. When they were very young (in fact Bryce was still in diapers), we set out on another massive adventure: llama-packing the 3,100-mile National Scenic Continental Divide Trail across the Rockies. In looking back on *that* feat, it was nearly as challenging as building a log home, but it also felt like it was just part of our life at the time—a goal that we worked hard to accomplish.

Building our log home gifted us with a unique vision for how we approach our lives and look ahead to our future and the goals that we set. With each new goal, we compare its level of difficulty, the stamina required, the amount of cooperation and communication needed to see it through, to what it took to build our log home. Goals like leading our small children across the wilderness, world-schooling them, growing an occupation like a chainsaw carver and a writer, living a voluntary, simplistic lifestyle, are all alternative life goals that Todd and

I were able to aim for and achieve because we first attempted and succeeded in building our log home all those years ago. It taught us how much we are truly capable of accomplishing, helped shape us into the people we are today, and gave us a life.

After we moved into our log home, Todd worked full-time on the house and property for another four years straight. He built Victorian screen doors, added the sunroom, the porch, and the deck. He went on to build a chicken house, llama shed, writing cabin/guest house, and a barn to support our homestead. He put in an orchard and a garden, and finally, a blacksmith shop. As a challenge to himself, Todd always tried to keep the cost of each outbuilding below $300. To do this, he incorporated recycled building materials and on the writing cabin and guest house, salvaged oak timbers from an old barn that he re-notched and chinked. Our log home is 2,500 square feet, which is not huge, but Todd's philosophy was he would rather build another outbuilding for a particular purpose than initially create a massive house when we were first learning how to build.

Although our log home does have indoor plumbing, we still live without central heat. We spend about twenty dollars a year for heat in chainsaw gas and oil, since we only burn three cords a year with our energy-efficient log home and we get the fuelwood off our twelve acres, from dead trees. In our orchard sits a solar shower, powered by the sun. Seeing fireflies, sunsets, and shooting stars as we walk back to the house wearing only a towel makes outdoor showering magical.

Even feeding our family is a creative act, for beyond our log home is our large garden, our orchard of more than twenty fruit trees, plus an extensive berry patch. We put up and preserve our organic food, make sausage from meat that we raise or animals we hunt, brew beer, and grow mushrooms on inoculated oak logs. Eating this way is like health and life insurance for our family, besides giving us the intense satisfaction of growing what we eat.

This lifestyle choice isn't only about living cheaply but becoming more connected to place, living lighter on the planet, and with more intent. We put considerable thought into designing and creating a life that brings us the most joy, but not necessarily the most money. Merely chasing money to buy things with no time to enjoy them made no sense to us. Our philosophy was that every purchase needs to be rated by comparing the amount of time and life we must give up in exchange for it.

In those early years, Todd made most of his living as a fine furniture maker and also filled our home with his projects, including steam-bent ladder back chairs, an oak pedestal table and a turned post bed, in which I was fortunate to deliver my son, Bryce, during his home birth. When Todd grew dissatisfied with the type of hardware available for his hand-crafted furniture, he enrolled in blacksmithing courses. His skill quickly blossomed from drawer pulls to ornate chandeliers, and he became a very talented blacksmith artist.

In the last twelve years, Todd has taken his carving skills, which he gained from cutting so many notches on our log home, coupled with his innate talent as an artist, to become an extremely talented and successful chainsaw carving artist. He loves to carve and creates and sells about 150 pieces a year. This highly honed skill was enhanced by just a two-hour lesson at an art school; otherwise he taught himself. Todd's specialty is animals, particularly raptors such as eagles and hawks. Living near Hawk Mountain Sanctuary, a world-famous sanctuary for migrating raptors, has increased his affection for the species and also his clients. In this very real sense, building our log home has gifted him with the most satisfying and successful livelihood.

I used the act of writing about building our log home as a way of practicing my craft as a writer. Although this book was first drafted and illustrated thirty years ago, it helped hone not only my skill but also my confidence as a writer. Our family's extensive travel over the years, both domestic and abroad, as well as our many outdoor adventures provided the fuel and fodder for me to become a travel writer. In the last twenty-five years, I've published over one thousand magazine articles and nine books. No matter where we travel in the world and how much beauty we are exposed to, returning to the sanctuary of our log home is always a joy. There is nothing like leaving a place to make you appreciate what you already have at home.

One of the greatest gifts resulting from building our home is the strong relationship that Todd and I share. The years we spent raising logs and raising walls were a crash course in understanding how we think, work, and relate to each other. We learned how to navigate life together, while still honoring our individual needs to pursue our own art, passions, hobbies, and callings.

Todd and I have never discussed our division of labor—our individual roles. Yet it has always worked. We figured it out early, back on the actual log home building site, and it has spread to encompass our entire lifestyle. We each embrace different jobs that need to be done in order to make our lifestyle work. We each choose tasks that we either enjoy more than the other or are better at doing. We came to an understanding and appreciation of what each person contributes in our own way in this shared life, but also value and respect each other's contributions.

We were then able to go on as a team in raising and educating our children in a unique way (traveling the world, going on big outdoor adventures, alternative learning), giving us the courage to follow our heart's desires and passions as opposed to what the rest of society was doing.

When our children were young, they did not think of their home as anything unusual. It was normal to them. Because of the openness of the design, we became accustomed to a shared home life and grew very close as a family. We used our home as a base for creating and learning. For many years, the kids homeschooled and then taught themselves. The children never saw a need for artificial stimulation from a television, but their library contained a huge number of books, while their desks held a massive and varied amount of art supplies. They wrote and performed plays, played musical instruments, made jewelry and all kinds of art, as they felt stimulated and encouraged to pursue creativity. Indeed, the log home surrounded them with beautiful, handmade things that their parents had created, from the massive log walls and soaring trusses, to Todd's handmade furniture, sculpture, and ironwork, to my landscape paintings, which adorn the log walls.

Todd and I were never ones to keep our log home and beautiful property all to ourselves. Rather, we sought out ways to share it. We have been hosting college students from universities in Pennsylvania and Maryland and leading a voluntary simplicity and sustainability workshop for the past three decades. Professors bring their students to our home knowing that they will benefit greatly from a hands-on visit to meet and talk to real "homesteaders." Visiting students hear how we built our log home and designed a life closely connected to the land and the natural world. This workshop's intent is to show students how they, too, can think outside the box, even if building a log home or creating a lifestyle like ours is not what they want to pursue. Rather our message for these young people is that they have the power to design *their* own lives. They also come to see that our philosophy of living a minimalist lifestyle is really about creating more in your life—more joy, more time, more connection.

While Todd and I were building our log home, we lived on the other side of the Appalachian Mountains in the National Park Service house located right on the Appalachian Trail. Part of our responsibility was hosting long-distance hikers who were en route from Georgia to Maine. After we moved into our log home, we still picked up hikers to offer a meal and shower, but they were a handful compared to the hundreds that we previously hosted each year.

Of particular note, however, were a group of veterans who in 2014 were hiking the trail to heal from their war trauma. Todd and I brought the five veterans to our log home and were so impacted by their journey, that a deep and lasting friendship developed between us. They inspired Todd and I to begin a 501(c)(3) nonprofit, River House PA, to aid veterans in their path toward healing through outdoor recreation. We have worked with multiple local US Department of Veterans Affairs (VA) hospitals and medical centers and, along with their recreational therapists, have led the veterans on hikes and paddles to show them how nature can not only bring peace to a soul but help heal its wounds. Nearly every event concludes with a visit to our log home for a campfire, a home cooked meal, and hand-cranked ice cream.

Todd and I created a large, comfortable space next to our log house, by the frog pond in the forest, in which the veterans can relax and decompress from the rigorous rehabilitation programs that they are enrolled in. As the veterans go around the fire, taking turns to express what it has meant for them to be in nature and share our wonderful log home and property, many shed tears of gratitude. This is the ultimate gift that our log home has returned to us, in exchange for all the hard work we have put into it: to be able to use our home to help heal those who need it the most, is the greatest gift of all.

Over the last three decades since our log home was built, we have experienced challenges that any couple or family can expect to encounter throughout their lives. But the lessons learned, and the relationship forged when we set log upon log, put a very strong foundation under us—not only for our marriage but for our entire family. Building our log home, truly showed us to how build an amazing life. As the Finnish proverb goes, *"Oma tupa, oma lupa,"* "One's own cabin, one's own freedom."

Appendix:
Log Home Building Basics

(Provided by Ron Brodigan and the Great Lakes School of Log Building)

If you are going out to the bush for building a log cabin or house, there is a presumption that you will have the following:

- 200 feet of hemp rope, 1" diameter, for setting up parbuckling on your building.
- An old pickup truck, or better yet, a cheap 1–2 ton flatbed, maybe a trailer or two.
- Several lengths of heavy ⅜" chain and maybe a choker cable (or chain) or two.
- Rakes and scoop shovels for cleaning up sawdust and debris.
- #2 shovels and picks for digging.
- Wheelbarrows for hauling debris and for mixing cement or concrete.
- Scrap logs for placing your building logs on to keep them off the ground.
- Scrap lumber for scaffolding, etc. Tarps for covering tools and stuff, or a temporary or permanent toolshed.
- Lot of nails and Torx screws and a battery-operated driver. Crowbars & various hammers etc.

- A camper or quickie plywood cabin for staying in while you build with logs.
- Water source for drinking and cleaning.
- Gasoline and diesel cans.
- Ladders, homemade or purchased.

Log Building Tools

(Provided by Ron Brodigan and the Great Lakes School of Log Building)

- Wood chisel. Two Cherries brand 20 mm with #3 curve.
- Mortise or framing chisel. 1, 1¼, or 2-inch.
- A mallet
- Drawknife. The best available is the 9" drawknife from Timber Tools/Buffalo Forge at $197. 1.800.350.8176 or www.timber-tools.com, or at Kingsbridge Supply.
- Log cleats, 2 sets or pairs—one pair consists of two cleats on a 30" rope.
- Peavey or Canthook (either will do). "Peavey" brand is superior. 4 or 5-foot handles are good. You will eventually have both for your own projects.
- Log scriber. 9-inch Ely scriber from Kingsbridge or Tamarack is one of the best available, in our opinion. Other brands, including the Robert Chambers scriber and the Veritas, are also excellent.
- Indelible pencils. 1 dozen, and lumber crayons.
- Axe. Scandinavian Forest axe by Gransfors-Bruks, if you want the world's best axe. Other small axes may do, but hatchets, in my opinion, are just plain dangerous since they are held in one hand, potentially risking the other, which might be holding something to be cut.
- Measuring tape. 25–50 foot. Also, small pocket tape (e.g., 10', 12') with both metric & English (if possible).
- Flat Mill Bastard File and flat sharpening stone.

- Chalk line with black chalk, and a hank (roll) of mason's line with line level.
- Any empty spray bottle (under your sink) for enhancing scribe pencil lines.
- Small torpedo level. A regular 24" level is also good. An Empire 24" level (#450-24 Speed Level) with graduations in English and metric and one flat (blade) edge **is the best ever for truss building and other uses.** (Not made anymore but occasionally available on Amazon & eBay for around $20.)
- 4–5-inch angle-grinder with separate rubber/plastic sanding backer and #24 or #36 grit discs. Be certain that the rubber or plastic backer fits your machine. The backer never comes in the box with the machine; it is always bought separately. Try putting it on at the store. If you have an incorrect backer, the sander is not useful. The best and safest angle-grinder I've found is a Paddle-Switch Makita, Model 955-7PB
- Heavy 100-foot extension cord—12 gauge is best (14 is OK).

Chainsaw

(Provided by Ron Brodigan and the Great Lakes School of Log Building)

- Purchase your saw from a bona fide chainsaw dealer in your home area.
- Stihl, Jonsereds, and Husqvarna brands are recommended.
- Arborist saws are not useful for log construction.
- Possibly the best saw for this course and your future log building—in terms of reliability, safety, noise, vibration reduction, parts/service availability, general usefulness, and long life—is the Stihl MS261 C-M, which is a medium-sized professional-level saw.
- For safety, noise, and reliability reasons, McCulloch, Homelite, Remington, Craftsman, Echo, and Poulan brands are not recommended.

- The chain specs for the Stihl MS261 are: Stihl 23RM3 if you have .050 bar slot gauge, Rapid-Micro Safety chain for .325 pitch.
- If you have .063 bar slot width, you need 26RM3 Rapid-Micro Safety chain.

Accompanying Tools

- Scrench (screwdriver-wrench combo), files, 2 old toothbrushes for cleaning. Saw should have 16" or 18" bar with .325 pitch. For log building the chain should be chipper or semi-chisel with rounded profile and should be an official green-linked safety chain, which Stihl terms "guard-link semi-chisel green chain." Saw should have at least the mechanical chainbrake.

Other Tools

- Toolbox or pail with tool bucket attachment.
- Claw hammer
- Framing square
- Handlebar gouge—a big favorite
- Pickaroon (or a hookaroon)
- Curved adze—the only useful ones seem to be from Tamarack or Kingsbridge Supply.

Safety Apparel

(Provided by Ron Brodigan and the Great Lakes School of Log Building)

- Hard hat, preferably with eye and ear protection. Warm liner for winter.
- Leather gloves for all tool use and sharpening. Also get a pair of heavy rubber-coated canvas work gloves for wet weather and for applying coatings to logs.
- First aid kit to keep handy while you are working on your log structure.

- Safety glasses or the face screen above. Disposable dust masks.
- Chainsaw-protective chaps or safety pants.
- Chainsaw-protective steel-toed Kevlar-lined boots. Steel-toes barely protect 1/6 of the foot from an axe or chainsaw, so the boots should be chainsaw-resistant and Kevlar-lined as well as having a steel-toe. Husqvarna or Labonville are recommended, either rubber or leather. Labonville (www.Labonville.com) has extremely comfortable US-made logging boots known as BOOTLAB9 Kevlar Safety Box Toe. Ser. no. is 24127 or 24128 (high or low heel). Husqvarna rubber or leather Kevlar-lined boots from a dealer are also acceptable. Ben Meadows Co. 800.241.6401 has the rubber type for around $100. The Log Home Store also has good rubber protective boots for $90+.
- Chainsaw-protective shirt. Special item developed in the 1990s by Ron in collaboration with Swedish Gransfors-Bruks Co. to provide arm, shoulder, and frontal trunk protection specifically for Great Lakes School courses. Washable blue denim. Available only at Tamarack, Log Home Store, or Kingsbridge. Caution: do not buy Stihl's orange shirt. It is not protective of anything except shoulders. After making sure it fits, wash your Gransfors-Bruks denim chainsaw shirt two or three times for extra comfort.
- Kneepads. Any kind. Easy on the knees for kneeling on scaffold or ground.

Resources

- Kingsbridge Supply. http://www.kingsbridgesupply.com. General log building and logging tools. The sole source for handlebar gouges and most everything.
- Magard Tools, Prince George, BC 250-962-9057. Full line of log and timber frame tools, including Chambers scribers and old Mackie scribers. www.logbuildingtools.ca/

APPENDIX: LOG HOME BUILDING BASICS

Books

- Chambers, Robert, *Log Construction Manual*, Log Cabin Publisher, "revised" 2016 edition only.
- Hand, Roger, *Building Your Own Low Cost Log Home*, Garden Way Publishing/Storey Publishing, North Adams, MA, 1985.
- Mackie, Allen, *The Owner-Built Log House*, Firefly Books, Richmond Hill, Ontario, Canada, 2001.
- Mackie, Allen, *Notches of All Kinds, Log Span Tables, Log House Plans*, Firefly Books, Richmond Hill, Ontario, Canada, 1997. (Note: Mackie's *Notches* is out of print and can be hard to locate, but there seem to be many in existence.)
- Mackie, Allen, *Building with Logs*, Firefly Books, Richmond Hill, Ontario, Canada, 1997
- Milne, Dan, *Handbook of Canadian Log Building*, Walker, Tom, *Building the Alaska Log Home*, Alaska Northwest Publishing Company, Portland, Oregon, 1983.
- *The International Log Builders Association's Effective Practices and Methods for Handcrafted Log Building*, (amply illustrated in color, 71 pages), North Orillia, Ontario, Canada, 2020.
- The ILBA website: *www.logassociation.org* will show you how to purchase it through Amazon for less than $30. Ron was on the committee of handcrafted builders around the continent who debated the issues and wrote this revision in 2010.

Schools

Cascadian School of Log Building and Design
PO Box 390
Rhododendron, Oregon 97049
Dave Rogers, Founder
david@cascadianlogschool.com

Dazian Joinery
Dai Ona, Founder
2947 Shuswap Rd. East

Kamloops, BC V2H 1T1
dai@daizen.com
250-573-1112

Salvage Sources

A directory of architectural salvage stores in the US:
https://www.oldhouseonline.com/interiors-and-decor/where-to-shop-for-architectural-salvage

Great places to buy architectural salvage:
https://www.bobvila.com/articles/1120-great-places-to-buy-architectural-salvage/

Glossary

adze. An axe-like tool with its blade at right angles to its handle, used to shape logs or timbers.

batter boards. Boards erected to show the proper height and corners for a concrete foundation.

block and tackle. An apparatus of pulley blocks and ropes used for hoisting heavy objects.

bracing. A diagonal support used to stiffen unstable walls of frames.

brick jointer. A hand tool used to imprint grooves in the mortar between bricks or blocks when the concrete is setting up.

brushing. Lightly swinging the chainsaw to remove wood.

buttering block. The act of troweling masonry cement onto cement blocks of bricks.

carving. Using the tip of the saw to remove wood.

chainsaw bar. Part of the chainsaw that the chain travels on.

chainsaw teeth. Part of the chainsaw that does the cutting, consisting of steel links held together by rivets that rotate around a guide bar.

chaps. Front leggings without a trouser seat worn to protect the fronts of the legs.

chinking. The process or materials used to fill gaps between horizontal wall logs.

chuck. A special type of clamp used in a rotating tool, like a drill, to hold a drill bit in tightly.

come-along. A hand-operated ratchet winch used for lifting or pulling heavy items like logs.

concrete forms. A wall or trench built to pour concrete into that holds the wet concrete in place.

concrete trough. A long, narrow, shallow receptacle for mixing concrete.

cricket. A small drainage-diverting structure on a roof, placed at the junction of the roof slope on an angle, like above a chimney.

cross bracing. Bracing that acts as a diagonal support used to stiffen unstable walls of frames.

derrick. A type of large crane used for hoisting and moving heavy objects.

divining rod. A forked tree branch that allegedly indicates where subterranean water is located, utilized by a dowser.

doorjamb. Two vertical pieces lining or framing the sides of a doorway, which are used for support.

dormer. An upright window that is built into a sloping roof.

dowsing. An ancient technique for searching for underground water, minerals, etc. that observes the motion of a pointer like a divining rod. Dowsers are thought to be sensitive to energy sources or waves.

draftsman's compass. A V-shaped device for drawing circles or an arc.

drain field. Also called a leach field, an area where wastewater percolates through a network of perforated pipes that are laid in underground gravel-filled trenches or permeable soil.

drawknife. A knife blade with handles on both ends that is drawn toward the user to remove wood.

fascia. The flat horizontal trim board around a roof's edge.

feathering. A technique using the back side of the chainsaw by lightly dragging it across a flat surface to make it smoother.

Finnish sauna. A traditional, wood-fired bath originating in Finland.

footers. The basis of a structure, usually made of concrete, which supports the foundation of a house.

flashing. A thin piece of impervious material that is used as a barrier at joints to prevent moisture from entering a structure.

flyway. The arched groove on the end of a log that extends beyond and outside the notch.

gable. The part of the wall that encloses the end of a pitched roof.

gin pole. A supported pole that uses pulleys or block and tackle on its upper end to lift loads.

green logs. Logs that were just cut, containing a lot of internal moisture that did not have the opportunity to season (dry) by evaporation.

grommets. An eyelet placed in a tarp or sheet to protect it from being torn and to allow a rope or a cable to pass through it.

groove. A long narrow rectangular slot that runs parallel to the wood grain.

hacksaw. A saw with a fine-toothed blade that is stretched in a frame and used for cutting metal.

hand-crank boat winch. A hand-powered hoisting machine with a drum around which a cable is wound to lift a load.

hone. To sharpen or smooth with a whetstone (fine-grained stone) for attaining a sharp edge on metal tools.

indelible pencil. A pencil containing dye in the lead that will enable it to write on wet or green logs/wood.

joist. A length of supporting material in a building, arranged in a parallel design from wall to wall, used to support a floor or a ceiling.

Kevlar chaps. Chaps made of Kevlar, a synthetic fabric made by DuPont Corp., the long fibers of which contain very high tensile strength and are cut-resistant.

knee walls. A short wall used to support the rafters in timber roof construction.

lateral groove. A longitudinal groove cut into a log enabling it to fit onto the log below.

lath. A thin flat strip of wood nailed to rafters to back and hang slate from.

log butt. The wide end of the log.

log dog. An iron bar, like a staple, which is capable of being driven into logs to secure and immobilize them.

log taper. To gradually become thinner.

mallet. A hardwood hammer weighing from 1½ to 2½ pounds, used for driving a chisel.

mortise and tenon. A simple yet strong woodworking joint, often used when the two connecting pieces of wood are at right angles. The tenon acts as a peg and the mortise acts as a slot or hole.

mud. Wet masonry concrete.

notch. A recess near the end of a log cut to accept the next log at a right angle.

parquet. Wood of contrasting colors or grain patterns worked into a mosaic, especially on floors.

peavey. A long wooden lever with a metal point and a hinged hook for moving logs.

pickaroon. An axe-length tool with a sharp point to aid in moving logs.

pike pole. A long pole pointed with a sharpened spike used for raising frames or applying pressure on a tree.

plumb and level bubble. A tiny pocket of air in a vial contained in an instrument which is used to find level/plumb on a board or a log. The tool is laced on the item and moved accordingly in order to get the bubble in the liquid-filled vial to be centered.

plumb bob. A conical bob of lead or other heavy material forming the weight at the end of a plumb line.

plumb line. A line such as a cord with a plumb bob attached on its lower hanging end used to determine verticality.

post and beam. A type of construction using a frame of large timbers, which are joined and pegged together, usually using mortise-and tenon-joinery.

powdered lime. Calcium oxide in a white caustic powdered form.

prove pit. A hole dug on a building site to check for soil drainage that will determine the type of septic system that needs to be built.

purlin. A horizontal log along the length of a roof, halfway between the ridge and the plate, used to support the rafters.

R-value. A building term used to measure how well certain building insulation materials can resist heat. The higher the R-value, the greater the insulation performance.

ratchet winch. A device used for lifting or pulling something heavy, with a friction break to give increased mechanical advantage when hauling on a rope or cable.

rebar. Shortened term for reinforcement bar—a metal rod used in concrete to add strength.

ridgeline/ridgepole. The topmost horizontal roof member spanning between the gable ends.

rigging system. A system of ropes, chains and tackle for moving logs.

S-hooks. Metal hooks in the shape of an S.

sawhorse. A rack or frame with legs used to support a piece of wood that is being sawed.

Scandinavian scribed fit. A method of log building where a scribe is used to fit the logs together originating in Russia then taught to the Scandinavians.

scarf. A long angle cut at the notch to make a tighter joint, and prevent the notch from opening up when settling.

scriber. A metal tool used to draw a line onto the log below. It has two, fluid-filled containers with bubbles—one for measuring plumb (up and down) and one for horizontal, and a slot for holding an indelible pencil.

scribing. To mark a log by drawing a line with a scribe so it matches the irregular surface of another log.

sewage enforcer. An inspector that enforces the building rules that dictate and approve septic systems.

skidder. A heavy vehicle or a machine for dragging logs out of a forest.

skidding sled. A makeshift sled used to drag logs.

skidding tong. A metal implement consisting of two arms that are fastened together and are hinged for seizing and dragging logs.

slate anvil. A metal "T" stake that is driven into a log stump and used to support a roof slate for cutting.

sledgehammer. A long heavy hammer wielded with both hands and used for heavy hitting

slick. A chisel with at least a 2½-inch blade. It is pushed by hand instead of being struck with a mallet.

spline. A narrow strip of wood placed in matching grooves cut in two adjacent pieces of wood to hold them together.

square. To make an edge or a corner straight.

street pavers. Bricks used to pave roadways.

striking. To smooth the wet masonry joint between bricks or concrete blocks using a tool called a brick jointer.

timber carriers. A wooden handle with metal tongs used by two people to carry a log.

transit. A surveying and building instrument (a tripod-mounted telescope) used to measure horizontal and vertical angles. It moves free to help a builder level a foundation or sill timbers.

vapor lock. A pocket of vaporized gasoline in the fuel line of an internal combustion engine that obstructs the flow of fuel.

woodworking plane. A carpenter's tool with an adjustable blade used to smooth or level wood.

yard of concrete. A measurement for concrete—three feet by three feet by three feet.

Acknowledgments

Over the course of the four years that we built our log home, there were fifty individual friends and family who came to lend a hand. Forty helpers were men, ten were women. Todd and I might still be building now, thirty years later, had you all not offered your expertise, time, and strong backs. Thank you for the bottom of our hearts. Special thanks goes to the heavy hitters: Frank and Lila Fretz, Mick Charowsky, Dave Walp, and Steve Gomez. And to our log building teacher, Ron Brodigan, you not only showed us how to build but showed us how to believe in ourselves too. Both were necessary. The greatest thanks goes to my wonderful husband Todd, who not only worked so hard to make this dream home come true, but continues to work to create a fabulous life for us, side by side.